The Best Places
To Kiss™
In the Northwest

(and the Canadian Southwest)

A Romantic Travel Guide

by Paula Begoun
Beginning Press

Other books in *THE BEST PLACES TO KISS . . .* Series

The Best Places To Kiss In Northern California — $9.95

The Best Places To Kiss In Southern California — $9.95

The Best Places To Kiss In New York City   — $9.95

Please send a check for the total price of each book ordered plus $1.50 shipping and handling for your entire order to:

Beginning Press
5418 South Brandon
Seattle, Washington 98118

Managing Editor: Paula Begoun
Art Direction: Constance Bollen & Steve Herold
Cover Design: Rob Pawlak
Typography: Lasergraphics
Copy Editor: Phyllis Hatfield
Printing: Bookcrafters
Contributors: Sherree Bykofsky, Julie Carpenter, Carina Langstraat

Copyright 1991 by Paula Begoun
Beginning Press, 5418 South Brandon
Seattle, Washington 98118
Third Edition: November 1990
1 2 3 4 5 6 7 8 9 10

The Best Places To Kiss™ is a registered trademark of Beginning Press
ISBN 1-877988-00-6

This book and any others in the series may be ordered directly from the publisher.

Please include $9.95 ($12.95 Canadian) plus $1.50 postage and handling.

Special Acknowledgments

To my dear sister Avis Begoun for the original idea for this series, my husband Moshe for his amorous, helpful research assistance, Debbie and Rick Pope for sharing their Portland home with me, and the innkeepers I met along the way who make traveling through the Northwest such a very special experience.

Dedication

To all the starry-eyed Northwesteners who offered their valuable, heartfelt suggestions and helped us find the kissing places included in this collection.

Publisher's Note

This book is not an advertising vehicle. As was true in all *The Best Places to Kiss* books, none of the businesses included here was told it was included in the final selection process; establishments were neither charged fees nor did they pay us; and no services were exchanged. This book is a sincere effort to highlight those special parts of the Northwest that are filled with romance and splendor. Sometimes those places are created by people, as in restaurants, inns, lounges, lodges, hotels, and bed & breakfasts. Sometimes those places are untouched by people and simply created by G-d for us to enjoy.

The publisher made the final decision about which locations to select for this collection. Please write to Beginning Press if you have any comments, suggestions or recommendations.

"As usual with most lovers in the city —
they were troubled by the lack of that
essential need of love — a meeting place."

Thomas Wolfe

> *"Love doesn't make the world go around —
> it's what makes the ride worthwhile."*
>
> **Franklin P. Jones**

TABLE OF CONTENTS

> *In literature, as in love,*
> *we are astonished at what*
> *is chosen by others.*
> André Maurois

KISSING 101

Is It Better To Kiss In The Northwest?

We ask a similar question in the introduction of each kissing guide, and each area has stirred a different answer. Before we answer such a provocative question for this new edition of the Northwest book, a bit of background is necessary: *The Best Places To Kiss In The Northwest* was the first book in this series of romantic travel guides. Beginning Press has since gone on to publish three others: *The Best Places To Kiss In Northern California, The Best Places To Kiss In Southern California,* and *The Best Places To Kiss In New York City.* (*The Best Places To Kiss In New England* will be available in the summer of 1991.) After all this lip-chapping research, we find it even easier to answer the question about the Northwest.

As publishers, it is important for us to confess our bias: we simply adore this glorious part of the world. More than any other area in the United States, the Northwest has a splendor and peacefulness that is apparent in almost every one of its localities. And along with the beauty of nature's handiwork, the people here have a style and attitude that are quietly conducive to intimacy and affection. A Northwest secret is, the more intimately acquainted you are with the earth, the more intimate you can be with each other. In short, it is not only better to kiss here, it is sheer ecstasy.

You Call This Research?

This book is the product of earnest interviews, careful investigation and close observation. Although it would have been nice, and from my viewpoint even preferable, kissing was not the major research method we used for selecting the locations listed in this book. (And you thought this was the hottest job in town, didn't you?) If smooching had been the determining factor, several inescapable problems would have developed. First, I assure you, we would still be researching and this book would be just a good idea, some breathless moments, random notes, overused credit cards and nothing more. And, depending on the mood of the moment, many kisses would have occurred in a lot of places that do not meet the requirements of this travel guide (which would have been fun, but not productive). Thus, for both practical and physical reasons, a more objective criterion had to be established.

How could we be certain that a particular place was good for kissing if we did not indulge in such an activity at every location? The honest, though boring, answer is that we used our reporters' instincts to evaluate the magnetic pull of each place visited. If during our visit we felt a longing for our special someone to share our discovery, we considered that longing to be as reliable as a thorough kissing evaluation. In the final analysis, we can guarantee that once you choose where to go from among the places listed, you will find some amount of privacy, a beautiful setting, a heart-stirring ambience and (generally) first-rate accommodations. Once you get there, what you do romantically is up to you and your partner.

How Important Is Location?

You may be skeptical about the idea that one location is more romantic than another. You may think, "Well, it isn't the setting, it's who you're with that makes a place special." And you'd be right. But aside from the chemistry that exists between the two of you without any help from us, there are some locations that can facilitate and enhance the chemistry, just as there are some that can discourage and frustrate the magic in the moment.

For example, a tender embrace and an impassioned kiss at the grocery store might be, for some, a rapturous interlude. But the other shoppers and the kids running down the aisle and the preoccupied clerk who dropped your eggs can put a damper on heart-throb stuff for most of us, even the most adoring. Yes, location isn't everything; but when a certain type of place combines with all the right atmospheric details, including the right person, the odds are undeniably better for achieving unhindered and uninterrupted romance.

With that in mind, here is a list of the things that were considered to be not even remotely romantic: olive green or orange carpeting (especially if it was mildewy or dirty); anything overly plastic or overly veneered; an abundance of neon (even if it was very art deco or very neo-modern); most tourist traps, particularly those with facilities for tour buses; overpriced hotels with impressive names or locations but mediocre accommodations; discos; the latest need-to-be-seen-in nightspot; and most places that encourage visits by families and children.

Above and beyond these unromantic location details, there is a small variety of unromantic behaviors that can negate the affection potential of even the most majestic surroundings. These are mood-killers every time: any amount of moaning over the weather (if you don't think rain and mist are romantic, you shouldn't be in the Northwest); creating a scene over the quality of food or service, no matter how justified; worrying about work; getting angry about traffic (even if it makes you miss a ferryboat); incessant back-seat driving, no matter how warranted; and groaning about heartburn and other related symptoms, no matter how annoying.

Romance Ratings

The three major factors that determined whether a place would be included here were:
1. **Surrounding splendor**
2. **Privacy**
3. **Tug-at-your-heartstrings ambience**

Of the three determining factors, "surrounding splendor" and "privacy" are fairly self-explanatory. "Heart-tugging ambience" can probably use some clarification. Ambience, by our definition, is not limited to four-poster beds covered with down quilts and lace pillows, or tables decorated with white tablecloths and nicely folded linen napkins.

Added to all that there must be a certain plushness or other engaging features that encourage intimacy and allow for continuous affectionate discussions. For the most part, ambience was rated according to degree of comfort and number of gracious appointments, as opposed to image and frills.

If a place had all three of the qualities listed above, its inclusion was automatic. If one or two of the criteria were weak or nonexistent, the other feature(s) had to be really incredible before the place could be recommended. For example, if a breathtakingly beautiful viewpoint was situated in an area inundated with tourists and families on vacation, the place was not included. On the other hand, if a fabulous bed & breakfast was set in a less-than-desirable location, it was included if and only if its interior was so wonderfully inviting and cozy that the outside world no longer mattered.

◆ *Romantic Note:* The Northwest is inherently a romantic place and it is also a huge geographic area. Often we found ourselves in an area with magnificent scenery but with few amenities of any kind — let alone romantic restaurants and inns. We were in a predicament: should we ignore a magnificent area because there aren't any facilities that can be recommended wholeheartedly, or should we relax our standards a bit and find decent (though not necessarily irreproachable) places where you can lay your heads down after a day of blissfully touring the countryside? We decided on the latter, and consequently you will read many entries that read something like "this isn't romantic but . . ." We know you won't be disappointed with our decision.

Kiss Ratings

If you've flipped through this book and noticed the miniature lips that follow each entry, you're probably curious about what they represent. Most other travel guides use a star system to rank the places they write about; for obvious reasons, we have chosen lips. The rating system notwithstanding, ALL the places listed in this book are wonderfully special places to be, all of them have heart-pleasing details and are worthwhile, enticing places to visit. The tiny lips indicate only our personal preferences and nothing more. They are a way of indicating just how delightfully romantic we found a place to be and how pleased we were with the service and environment during our visit. The number of lips awarded each location indicates the following:

	Romantic Possibilities
❖	Very Romantic
❖❖	Magical
❖❖❖	Irresistible
❖❖❖❖	Sublime

Cost Ratings

There are also ratings to help you determine whether your lips can afford to kiss in a particular restaurant, hotel or bed & breakfast (almost all of the outdoor places are free of charge or there is a minimal fee for parking and entrance). The price listing for overnight accommodations is always based on double occupancy (otherwise there wouldn't be anyone to kiss). Eating establishment prices are based on a full dinner for two, excluding liquor, unless otherwise indicated. Because prices and business hours change, it is always advisable to call ahead to each place you consider visiting, so that your lips do not end up disappointed.

Restaurant Rating

Very Inexpensive	Under $25
Inexpensive	$25 to $45
Moderate	$50 to $75
Expensive	$80 to $100
Very Expensive	$105 and up

Lodging Rating

Very Inexpensive	Under $65
Inexpensive	$70 to $85
Moderate	$90 to $115
Expensive	$120 to $155
Very Expensive	$160 to $195
Unbelievably Expensive	$200 and up

What If You Don't Want To Kiss?

Some people we interviewed resisted the idea of best-kissing locales. Their resistance stemmed from expectation worries. They were apprehensive that once they arrived at the place of their dreams, they'd never get the feeling they thought they were supposed to have. They imagined spending time setting up itineraries, taking the extra time to get ready, making the journey to the promised land and, once they were there, not being swept away in a flourish of romance. Their understandable fear was: what happens if nothing happens?

Having experienced those situations more than once in my life, I empathize, but I'm prepared with solutions. To prevent this anti-climactic scenario from becoming a reality, and to help you survive a romantic outing, consider these suggestions: when you make decisions about where and when to go, pay close attention to details; talk over your preferences and discuss your feelings about them. For some people there is no passion associated with fast pre-theatre dinners which are all but inhaled, or with walking further than expected in overly high, high heels, or with finding a place closed because its hours have changed. Also keep in mind the difficulties of second-guessing traffic patterns. My strong recommendation, although I know this one can be tricky, is not to schedule a romantic outing too tightly or you will be more assured of a headache than an affectionate interlude.

A few miscellaneous suggestions: do not discuss money, family or the kids, keep your eyes on what's on your plate, not on his or hers; if you have a headache, take some aspirin now and not later; and regardless of how good-looking the person at the next table is, remember that such distractions are never considered to be in romantic good taste. How different factors might affect your lips, not to mention your mood, is something to consider before you head out the door, not after.

In spite of all that, it is important to remember that part of the whole experience of an intimate time together is to allow whatever happens to be an opportunity to let affection reign. Regardless of what takes place, that is what is romantic. For example, remember the incredibly intense scene in the film *Body Heat*, where Kathleen Turner is standing in the hall and William Hurt smashes through the door (even though it appears to be unlocked) and rushes into her waiting arms, tumbling them both to the floor? Well, how romantic would it have been if Kathleen had started fretting about having to clean up the broken glass, get the door fixed and repair her torn underwear? Or remember the scene between Kevin Kostner and Susan Sarandon in *Bull Durham*, where he throws his full cereal bowl against the wall, cleans the kitchen table with a sweep of his arm and then picks Susan up and throws her passionately on the table? Well, how romantic would that have been if Kevin had started complaining about the broken china in his hair and the spilled milk running down his arms? Get the idea?

So, if the car breaks down, the waiter is rude to you, your reservations get screwed up, or both of you tire out and want to call it a day, you can still be endearing and charming. It really only takes an attitude change to turn any dilemma into a delight.

The Most Romantic Time To Travel

The Northwest is truly so spectacular, it's hard to imagine any time of the year or the week that would not be romantic. Each season and hour has its own special joy: winter skiing, fireplaces on a chilly day, the warmth of summer, mesmerizing fall sunsets, the rebirth of nature in the melting wet spring. Even in overcast conditions, if you pre-pare properly there is no reason to postpone investigating the splendor that hovers around every turn in the Northwest. So don't be one of those couples who waits until summer to travel and then decides not to go because it might be too crowded. Oh, and about the rain — it does. Enough said.

> *"How lucky I am that love ran out to meet me with open arms and courted me with romance."*
> **Sheila Pickles**

BRITISH COLUMBIA

◆ Vancouver Island & Gulf Islands ◆

VANCOUVER ISLAND

Vancouver Island is accessible by ferryboat from Anacortes, Washington, or from downtown Seattle on the Stena Line ships. From British Columbia it is accessible by ferry from Tsawwassan Bay, just south of Vancouver, from Horseshoe Bay in West Vancouver, and from Westview, on the Sunshine Coast due north of Vancouver.

Traveling to Vancouver Island is an unconditional romantic must, simply because there is everything here that two people in love could want to share. This huge land mass is resplendent with deep forest, an English-style city, miles upon miles of wilderness, rugged coast, fishing villages, sandy white beaches, rustic lodges, quaint bed & breakfasts, magnificent bed & breakfasts, and a mountain range that spans its nearly 300-mile length.

It was a struggle to narrow down the entries for this island. Almost every acre is distinctively attractive, interesting and loaded with great places for romantic interaction. The north-central section is mostly uninhabited and thus full of untouched mountain terrain, wildlife and pristine scenery. The eastern coastal areas are marbled with long lazy beaches, densely forested hills and meadows. The west coast is entirely wilderness except for the congenial fishing villages of Tofino and Ucluelet. The city of Victoria, on the southern tip of the island, presents a great contrast to all these natural wonders; there is old-world architecture and sightseeing paraphernalia on every corner. Along the southwestern coast, the unspoiled wilderness is again apparent in rocky beaches and extensive forestland.

The great variety of terrain and culture may make it difficult for you to decide where to go first. But at least one thing is clear — you have to start by ferryboat. For information, fares and schedules, contact either the **British Columbia Ferries**, (604) 669-1211, or the **Washington State Ferries**, (206) 464-6400.

CAPE SCOTT PARK

From the Nanaimo ferry dock take Highway 19 north to Port Hardy. Just south of town, follow the poorly marked logging road for 28 miles. At the end of the road, you'll pass a government-run meteorology station as you proceed to the parking area at the head of the trail. A very short climb reveals the path.

Cape Scott is on the northwest tip of Vancouver Island and feels like the end of the world. It is accessible only by a miserable, dusty gravel-and-stone logging road. The park is not all that far from Port Hardy, but because of the road's condition, you'll need longer to get here than you'd think from just looking at a map. When you finally arrive, you will be ecstatic that you survived the ordeal, since this park is the epitome of wilderness.

At the beginning of the hiking trail, you'll make a dreamlike transition from the gravel-pit road to a land filled with the elfin spirits of nature. A flat walkway of wood planks is the only sign of civilization, including people, you're likely to see all day; you are guaranteed privacy.

From the trailhead, you meander for two miles through trees wardrobed in moss and streamered with sunlight. Your path finally opens onto an enormous sand-laden horseshoe bay called San Josef, which you can claim exclusively for yourselves. The waves breaking on the beach fill the air with a rhythmic pounding. The U-shaped boundary is marked by forested hills where very few people have gone before. At the end of the trail be sure to mark where you leave the trail or it will be tricky to find that spot again.

◆ **Romantic Note:** Because Cape Scott is a remote location, you should acquire a detailed map and complete information from the visitor center in Port Hardy before you head out there.

STRATHCONA PARK & LODGE, Campbell River
P.O. Box 2160
(604) 286-2008
Moderate

Just north of Campbell River, take Highway 28 west for 30 miles to the lodge.

When I arrived at Strathcona Lodge, having driven along a winding mountain road into the core of Vancouver Island to get there, I walked up to the reception desk and the first words out of my mouth were, "What sort of lodge is this?" The answer to that question is, "Like no other lodge on earth!" The red hewn-log buildings of the lodge are set at the edge of a crystal-clear mountain lake encircled by an astounding collection of overlapping snowcapped peaks. Strathcona is without question a visual paradise. There are also no other facilities around for miles, and that has an enchantment all its own.

The staff of Strathcona Lodge are dedicated to introducing all who venture into their realm to the mysteries and excitement of the outdoors. They offer guided instruction for any mountain and water activity you could wish for: kayaking, rappelling from cliffs, glissading down glaciers, wildlife hiking, canoeing, fishing, sailing and camping. Their brochure lists a rare selection of packaged challenges for all ages and skill levels.

I know — that all sounds great but not necessarily romantic, unless of course you're Paul Bunyan on a date, or parents trying to keep your kids busy. But after I explored the lodge and the rustic cabins around the lake, observed the three hearty meals served family-style daily, and noticed that the lodge does offer a honeymoon package, I was convinced that this was an extraordinary place for an outdoor-loving couple. There is nothing quite like it anywhere else in the Northwestern U.S. or Southwestern Canada. For that reason alone, your outdoor fantasies will be fulfilled at Strathcona Lodge.

PAINTER'S LODGE RESTAURANT
AND LOUNGE, Campbell River

1625 MacDonald Road
(604) 286-1102
Moderate to Expensive

Just north of Campbell, turn right on MacDonald Road and follow the signs to Painter's Lodge.

This is another one of those places to which my husband insisted I award a four-lips rating—we often disagree on these kind of resorts. But as I've said before, and repeated several times to myself between 5 A.M. and 9 A.M., on a rocking boat, in the rain, out in the middle of a channel with no fish in sight—half of the battle is in considerately sharing what the other person thinks is romantic, no matter how wrong he or she might be.

Painter's fishing lodge is an angler's delight and has been for over 60 years. Canadians and Californians alike have flocked here to test their patience and skill. Due to a fire a few years back, the lodge has been entirely rebuilt, and the result, for the most part, is enticing and elegant. Some of the accommodations are still hotel-basic, but the rooms in the main lodge are really quite nice. None of that matters when the agenda is hooking a coho or king salmon, but it's generally disappointing for more intimate activity. However, the glass-enclosed fireside lounge, with its huge stone fireplace and comfortable seating, is a prime place to revitalize yourselves for another go-around after a few hours out on the Strait fighting off the dogfish and weeds.

Dinner in the main restaurant, framed by the same floor-to-ceiling windows as the lounge, is surprisingly elegant, with china, linens, formal service and impressive menu selections. The food was good, though given the effort of the staff, it should have been great.

THE OLD HOUSE RESTAURANT, Courtenay   ❦❦

1760 Riverside Lane
(604) 338-5406
Inexpensive to Moderate

As you approach the town of Courtenay, heading north along Highway 19, turn west at the first major intersection, which is the 17th Street Bridge. Then turn right again onto Riverside Lane, the road just before the river. The restaurant will be the first house on your left.

As you drive up to the eye-catching rustic mansion that is The Old House Restaurant, you'll be impressed by its rugged architecture and its garden setting. Willow trees and thick green lawn fill the backyard where outdoor dining is accompanied by the flow of the Powell River. (The nearby log-processing factory is often in full swing during lunchtime, but it wasn't as much of a distraction as I'd feared.)

This well-known Vancouver Island spot is an enjoyable place to dine. There are several very pretty rooms, each one dominated by a beach-stone fireplace framed by wood mantels. Antique furnishings and leaded-glass windows reflect warmth and gentility. The food is really quite good and the service, for the most part, is attentive and efficient, though sometimes strained when the place is busy. Unusual fresh ingredients placed among more standard items are the hallmarks of the kitchen. Pumpkin pasta, smoked goose, quail and venison are a few of the rare finds on this interesting menu. Certainly, if you find yourselves traveling through Courtenay on your way to the northern end of the island, this will be a fulfilling place to visit.

◆ *Romantic Alternative:* Near The Old House Restaurant is **LA CREMAILLIERE**, 975 Comox Road, (604) 338-8131 (Moderate to Expensive). Everyone I talked to said this was the most romantic restaurant on the entire island — well, at least outside of Victoria. The comments ranged from "incredibly intimate atmosphere" to "superior French cuisine with a fresh Northwest flare." My heart and appetite were more than stimulated, though unfortunately that's as far as it went. Their hours are brief, Wednesday through Sunday only, and my kissing partner and I were only in Courtenay Monday and Tuesday. So this is one of the few places I'm including based solely on reputation and interview. If you're in this area and decide to find out about La Cremailliere for yourselves, let me know what you think—I'd appreciate the information.

◆ *Romantic Suggestion:* Twenty-five minutes from Courtenay is the summer chair lift of **FORBIDDEN PLATEAU**, 2050 Cliff Avenue, Courtenay, (604) 334-4744, open June 5 through September 5. As you dangle above the golden land below, you can study the scenic Comox Valley, the Strait of Georgia and the Beaufort Mountain Range.

AVALON BY THE SEA, Parksville
1427 Bay Drive
(604) 248-5866
Moderate

From the Island Highway turn west on Northwest Bay Road to Terrien Road. Turn left, and then turn left again on Bay Road to the inn.

What a find — and what a shame that there are only three rooms in this enchanting, consummate bed & breakfast. The tree-lined driveway takes you past manicured fields where grazing horses adorn the landscape. As you circle around and up to the 7,500-square-foot home, on one side of the road you'll notice immaculate stables that are available for rent if you happen to have your own steed in tow. On the other side you'll see a heated swimming pool, complete with cabanas and patio. Inside, the three rooms are located in their own private wing of the main residence, with access to an unbelievable Grecian-style spa and sauna room and game suite complete with fireplace, stereo and television. All the units are exceptionally comfortable and uniquely laid out, each with an assortment of sea views, vaulted ceilings, private decks and soaking tub built for two. You may want to take advantage of this place soon, before it becomes impossible to get a reservation.

TIGH-NA-MARA, Parksville
R.R. #1
(604) 248-2072
Expensive

Just off Highway 19, on the east side of the road a few miles north of downtown Parksville.

If there were awards for impossible-to-figure-out names of restaurants and lodgings, this one would take the prize (though I have since learned that *tigh na mara* means "house by the sea" in Scottish Gaelic). If there were awards for excellence in resort accommodations, setting, views and dining facilities along the coast of Vancouver Island, Tigh-Na-Mara would walk away with an honorable mention at the very least.

There is so much here to praise. The clusters of log cabins are interspersed among pinery and red-barked trails. They have roomy interiors with broad stone fireplaces that keep things glowingly warm. The restaurant, set in a log mansion with a country-polished interior, is a fine place to enjoy a rich dining experience. They pay attention to comfort, and serve delectable fresh continental dishes, hearty breakfasts and lunches.

And then there are the recently added suites that lord it over the shoreline. These units were created with lovers in mind. The sliding glass door to your private deck opens onto a ringside view of the shore. Inside, the extensive living room has a fireplace, a hot tub and a silky new comforter for the queen-size bed. All in all, even though the name might be strange, the place itself has a seductive pull that can't be ignored.

◆ *Romantic Warning:* All of the cabins and rooms at Tigh-Na-Mara are set mostly in woods and, as a result, the interiors tend to be a bit on the dark side. Not a problem unless you were counting on bright sun-filled rooms. Many properties along the Island Highway, including Tigh-Na-Mara, are undergoing condominium conversion and development. Some of the rooms in the new wing are presently being sold. I don't think that will affect your stay here, but only time will tell.

◆ *Romantic Suggestion:* I believe that breakfasts are romantic — that is, if they are leisurely, somewhat stylish and accompanied by a resplendent view and a significant other. **HERON'S RESTAURANT** in the **BAYSIDE INN HOTEL**, Parksville, 240 Dogwood Street, (604) 248-8333 (Moderate) meets my qualifications. Even though the Bayside Inn is in essence just a hotel, with very nice hotel-like rooms and amenities, its restaurant is a three-tiered showcase with all the right touches to make brunch here a must.

TOFINO

From Highway 4 at Parksville, head west 75 miles across the center of the island to the water. Where the road dead-ends, follow the signs north to Tofino.

The 75-mile trip west on Highway 4 across the central mountains of Vancouver Island takes you to the remote side of the island. For the last few miles of this panoramic drive, the rocky coast chaperones you as you descend to sea level. When you finally reach road's end, the highway will split: one road forks north to Tofino, the other south to Ucluelet. Both towns are basically fishing villages and whale-watching ports of call. They also pride themselves on being non-commercial places where you can charter boats for fishing and water tours. But for heart-stealing pursuits, Tofino is your destination.

Tofino is what a small town should be — unpretentious, with amiable, unruffled streets and neighborhoods set like constellations along the volatile, rocky oceanfront and the marinas of the calm inner bay. Every corner of it provides an escape from the madding crowd. Along the main road into Tofino there are several waterfront resorts that line the shore and have unobstructed views of the beach and ocean. In town there are a few basic shops and casual restaurants. Nothing here gets in the way of the scenery. Get close, kick back and discover that you're in a place where time floats by to a melody you can learn to hum together.

◆ *Romantic Option:* Along the west coast, between Tofino and Ucluelet, **LONG BEACH** and **CHESTERMAN BEACH** offer an abundance of everything that restless surf-lovers could want. These locations are defined by rocky cliffs, smooth white-sand beaches, and forested picnic and hiking areas adjacent to the shoreline. The romantic possibilities are many: you can relax, walk along the extensive beach, hike through the forest bordering the shore, or seek the water for a salty frolic.

♦ *Romantic Note:* The tourist season here is so brief and intense (mostly in July and August), and the best accommodations so difficult to come by, you may want to consider another, less popular, season for your visit to this area. During the winter and fall it will seem that the two of you have the place to yourselves.

HOT SPRINGS COVE, Tofino

Hot Springs Adventures
320 Main Street
(604) 725-4222
Expensive

Hot Springs Adventures is one of many boat charters that can take you to Hot Springs Cove. Call for reservations and directions to the marina where you meet the boat.

Coastal wilderness is normally accessible only to those who own a seaworthy vessel that they can navigate along remote, often dangerous shores. But those people fortunate enough to find themselves in Tofino can take advantage of the daily round-trip boat excursions to Hot Springs Cove — and what a trip it is! After leaving the marina, you travel for an hour and a half amid the exquisite scenery of Clayoquot Sound as you head north for Shelter Inlet. Once you dock, you must hike for a bit through lush forest until you see the steaming mists of the cove. The warm, cascading water spills over rocky formations into a series of natural pools. As you soak away the last bits of tension in your neck and shoulders, lean back and watch the ocean waves crash onto the nearby shore. This natural shower is bound to be one you'll never forget.

◆ **Romantic Note:** You have to bring your own water or drinks to the cove, because water supplies are limited and at times altogether nonexistent. Should you desire to stay overnight and treat yourself to an early-morning rinse in the springs, there are campgrounds a short distance from the dock and there is also the newly built **HOT SPRINGS COVE LODGE**, (206) 725-4222. The six self-contained housekeeping units here will make you feel as if you're homesteading, except for the satellite-fed TV in your room. This touch of civilization seems out of place up here, but then, no one said you have to turn it on. We threw a blanket over ours and were thoroughly pleased with our entire stay.

OCEAN PACIFIC WHALE CHARTERS, Tofino
Box 590
(604) 725-3919
Moderate

Call Ocean Pacific for reservations and directions to the marina where you meet your boat. The height of the whale migration season is in March and April, though there are resident whales here in all seasons.

Take it from a skeptic — whale-watching is romantic. Imagine yourself and your loved one staring out from your open Zodiac boat at the Pacific Ocean lined with cliffs and forested islands haloed in colors of deep, verdant green. The coolness of the morning air swirls around you and you squeeze each other close for protection against the chill. You both slowly scan the calm, flowing blue motion and your thoughts are filled with the vastness before you. Then suddenly, in the distance, breaking the stillness of a sun-drenched winter day, a spout of water explodes from the ocean surface followed by a giant arching black profile. After an abrupt tail slap, all is stillness once again. Believe me, if you're not sitting next to someone you care about, you're likely to grab the person nearest you and yell, "Wow, look at that!"

Maybe it's the excitement of knowing that such an immense, powerful creature can glide so effortlessly through the water with playful agility and speed. Or it could be the chance of "connecting" with a civilized mammal that knows the secret depths of the aquatic world we can only briefly visit and barely understand. Whatever the reason, the search is one you need to share with someone special. Together you can contemplate what to anyone's way of thinking is surely a miracle.

OCEAN VILLAGE BEACH RESORT, Tofino
Box 490, Hellesen Drive
(604) 725-3755
Inexpensive to Moderate

On Highway 4 two miles south of Tofino, look for the sign on the west side of the road pointing the way to the resort.

There is nothing fancy about the 24 handsome, cedar-wood cabins that make up the accommodations of Ocean Village, but the view, location and privacy are another story. Eight of these units are individual huts stationed in a row on McKenzie Beach. The entrance to each of these private residences is a sliding glass door that faces the sand, wind and waves. Beachcombing, whale watching, hunting for seashells, building sand castles, playing in the surf, or listening to the waves lapping against the shore are some of the more strenuous activities you can find within inches of your door, and for miles in either direction. This place may not be fancy, but who needs fancy when you have a front yard like the one at Ocean Village?

◆ *Romantic Option:* Down the beach from Ocean Village is **CRYSTAL COVE BEACH RESORT**, Box 559, Tofino, (604) 725-4213, (Inexpensive), set on a quiet inlet next to McKenzie Beach. The log cabins here are lovely and well worth the stay if units 1, 2 or 3 are available. The resort is much like Ocean Village, except that these three units are charming, complete with fireplaces and cozy interiors that make for some of the best snuggling you'll uncover in Tofino.

CHESTERMAN'S BEACH BED & BREAKFAST,
Tofino

1345 Chesterman's Beach Road
(604) 725-3726
Moderate

Call for reservations and directions.

Oceanfront bed & breakfasts are a treat, for two predictable reasons. First, the proximity to the ocean is enthralling, and second, the delectable morning meal is enhanced wonderfully when an endless shoreline happens to be the backdrop. As you sit on the deck you can feel the breeze lift the sea air all around you. The cool mist tingles against your cheek, and as you sip hot fresh coffee the steam briefly warms your face. After breakfast a sentimental stroll, hand in hand through the surf, makes a great dessert.

Chesterman's is just such a bed & breakfast. There are three rustic units here — a large cabin with a private yard, a window-framed, second-story room with a balcony adjacent to the house, and a two-bedroom section on the lower level — all with private entrances. Each of these units is a viable option for a romantic sojourn in this part of the world, especially since all you need is each other and endless majestic scenery.

◆ *Romantic Suggestion:* The **BLUE HERON SEAFOOD RESTAURANT**, at the Weigh West Marine Resort, 634 Campbell Street, (604) 725-3277 (Moderate) is a great place to dine and watch the comings and goings of this busy sport-fishing marina. The view of Clayoquot Sound is at times still and calm, and at others bustling and exciting, depending on how many spring salmon have been caught. Don't expect an intimate repast here, just fresh food and a dazzling outdoor view of Tofino.

WICKANINNISH RESTAURANT, Ucluelet
Box 946
(604) 726-7706
Inexpensive to Moderate

Fifteen miles south of Tofino, on Highway 4, look for signs on the west side of the road that will direct you to the restaurant and interpretive center.

This is not your typical kissing place. Wickaninnish is the name of an outstretched beach with hundreds of weathered logs strewn like toothpicks along the shore. There is also a large wood building, with the same name, that houses an information center, a museum of Indian culture and a restaurant located on the edge of the sandy shore. The information center and museum, together known as the Interpretive Centre, are educational points of interest but hardly romantic, unless of course you want to kiss an artifact. The restaurant, on the other hand, is exceptionally romantic, particularly during off-season when the tourists are home waiting patiently for summer.

The restaurant is encircled by windows that showcase the beach and the ever-changing status of the shore. Threatening winter storms, dramatic high tides and motionless summer days create a changeable landscape that is at one moment languid and silent and the next violent and thundering. Regardless of what excitement nature is providing, Wickaninnish Restaurant will serve you gracious meals while you sit back and watch the show.

◆ *Romantic Note:* After lunch, weather permitting, Wickaninnish is a perfect place to hike along the beach or through the woods behind the back of the building. When you're done, return to the restaurant and drink a toast to the day you shared together.

CROW AND GATE, Ladysmith
Yellow Point Road
(604) 722-3731
Inexpensive

About three miles north of Ladysmith, on the Island Highway, turn right on Cedar Road and then turn right at the second entrance to Yellow Point Road. Travel for one mile to the restaurant, on the right side of the road. There are signs along Island Highway that will help guide you.

Among the pines, nestled in the rolling meadows of the countryside, protected by a rose arbor and spiced with rustic appeal, you'll find the ambience of another era in an English-style pub called the Crow and Gate. The setting of this cottage, on the pastoral east coast of Vancouver Island, provides a refuge to weary, hungry travelers looking for a place to have dinner and mellow out. Here you'll find restful pleasure as you take your tea or ale at a table near the stone hearth and let the evening linger on. The food is traditional British fare, with the accent on fresh, hearty and friendly. So snuggle close together and watch the embers flicker and glow in the dimly lit room as you wait for the innkeeper to fetch your afternoon or evening meal.

YELLOW POINT LODGE, Ladysmith
R.R. 3
(604) 245-7422
Moderate to Expensive

Call for reservations and directions to the lodge.

This is one place where I made reservations to return before I even left, it is that inviting and serene. While you are here, there is no need to do anything more strenuous than deciding what to wear to the three family-style meals and the three teas served daily in the handsome main lodge.

Why the hurry to sign up again? Because it is almost impossible to get a reservation. This popular B.C. getaway is well known for several reasons: its remote location with extensive beachfront and secluded coves bordered by 180 acres of forest; its attentive staff; its delicious meals; and its ability to truly relax you. This is a desirable, beautiful place for the heart, mind and soul.

The lodging choices here are eclectic. The best ones for romantic interaction are the new log cabins that line the shore, tucked among pines and hidden from view. There are more rustic accommodations scattered around the extensive property (in assorted price ranges). But you'll find that the real question to ask at Yellow Point Lodge is not "Where shall we stay?" but "When can we come back?"

GROVE HALL ESTATE, Duncan

6159 Lakes Road
(604) 746-6152
Moderate

Call for reservations and directions.

When we approached this poorly marked bed & breakfast we almost changed our minds and turned back. The entrance was rather eerie, like something out of an Edgar Allan Poe story. A cattle grate shook our car as ominous, ancient oak trees bowed over the driveway and almost entirely blocked the sun. Thank goodness I've learned never to turn back. By now I know there may always be something stupendous waiting on the other side of a dubious facade. Grove Hall once again proved the point.

At the end of this long, strange, access drive was a magnificent turn-of-the-century Tudor mansion set on 17 acres of gardens, sweeping lawns and accessible lakefront. There was nothing dark or strange about this place. Every corner and each detail was interesting and unique. The interior was a renovated masterpiece filled with amazing antiques, a luxurious living room, stately billiards chamber that has to be seen to be believed, formal dining area where an appropriately regal breakfast is served each morning, and exotic, sensuous guest suites. The Singapore Room has a huge, handcarved Chinese wedding bed with a view of the lake and gardens. The Indonesia Suite, with its own sitting room, has art pieces and batiks from that part of the world and a private balcony overlooking lake and garden. The Siamese Room has — you guessed it — twin beds and a private balcony set above the gardens.

If there is a flaw in this picture-perfect retreat, it can only be the shared bathroom facilities, though there are three available and they are each lovely. In my estimation, this is a small sacrifice to make for the rest of what you will gain at Grove Hall Estate.

◆ *Romantic Suggestion:* While waiting in line for a ferryboat, I got into a conversation with the couple in front of me who were from the town of Duncan. As is my way, I asked them where they would go for a romantic dinner in Duncan. Without hesitation they said that they had spent every wedding anniversary for the past seven years at **THE QUAMICHAN INN**, 1478 Maple Bay Road, (604) 746-7028 (Moderate). After I sought out this place I discovered why this couple kept on returning. Set on a knoll overlooking the Cowichan Valley, the restaurant is located on the lower level of a charming Tudor home. There are three cozy dining areas here, each with a glowing fireplace. The eclectic menu was interesting and worth a return visit to try the dishes we missed. Even if it's not your anniversary, the inn is a place for any special event you create. (There are bed & breakfast rooms upstairs, but these are not anywhere near the quality of the restaurant.)

FAIRBURN FARM COUNTRY MANOR, Duncan
R.R. #7, Jackson Road
(604) 746-4637
Moderate

Call for reservations and directions to the farm.

Fairburn Farm Country Manor has one of the most beautiful rural settings I have seen. The cow-pasture-type impressions I've had about farms will never be the same. As the innkeeper gave me a tour, I found myself staring off in the distance, unable to concentrate on anything but the rolling green hills, flawless forested grounds, sweeping fields, and gardens of floral brilliance.

After all of that, unfortunately, the bed & breakfast accommodations were a bit too much on the rustic side to qualify as romantic getaways. The rooms are really more family-oriented and the bathrooms are shared and down the hall. But on the chance that the restaurant has extra seatings for lunch or dinner, Fairburn Farm is a must for country-food lovers who find themselves near the town of Duncan. Most of the food is produced or raised on the farm, including the lamb and veal, and the rare treats like fresh-churned butter, stone-ground wheat bread, real maple syrup and homemade jams soothe and satisfy in a way store-bought fare never can.

PINE LODGE FARM BED & BREAKFAST, Mill Bay
3191 Mutter Road
(604) 743-4083
Inexpensive

Call for reservations and directions to the farm.

A 25-mile pilgrimage north of Victoria will place you here, in a serene countryside encompassed by welcome quiet. This eight-bedroom manor has an impressive white-pine exterior with an interior that is equally fascinating in its handsome detail and presence. A spacious sitting-room with an enormous stone fireplace is surrounded by the second-floor balcony, where the guestrooms are situated. The rooms are outfitted with antiques of superior workmanship and design. Any of the suites will prove to be a nurturing hideout, but the rooms with a view of the fields, the Strait of Georgia and the islands are ideal. Speaking of nurturing, breakfast is a last-you-all-day enterprise prepared with fresh eggs and homemade preserves, so be ready with an appetite to match.

DEER LODGE MOTEL, Mill Bay
R.R. 1 Island Highway
(604) 743-2423
Very Inexpensive

Just north of Mill Bay, on Highway 1, on the east side of the road.

If I were giving awards for the best bargain place to kiss besides the out-of-doors, Deer Lodge would win hands down. This isn't a fancy renovation or innovative new construction; in fact, the front of the building, which is most unattractive, resides directly on the main highway. There aren't even any four-color brochures to extol the lodge's character and value. According to the innkeeper, people just keep coming back. I'm certain the return rate is due in part to the enchanting views from the grand bay windows of the rooms that open out to the water and mainland. It is also due to the large, cushy suites, most with fireplaces and all with complete kitchens. The units are set facing away from the road, with a manicured lawn and gardens sweeping down the hillside to the view just beyond.

This location is one I consider a prize, because Vancouver Island can be as expensive as it is beautiful. At Deer Lodge you can have the beauty without the expense, in easygoing style and comfort.

◆ *Romantic Options:* **THE DUTCH LATCH RESTAURANT**, P.O. Box 26, Malahat, (604) 478-1880 (Moderate to Expensive) is just down the road a bit from Deer Lodge and you'd think it would also suffer from being right on Highway 1, with all its tourist-trap leanings. Yet inside, this is an adorable restaurant with a wonderful wood-framed fireplace, charming country design and tasteful touches all around — and even that isn't the reason to stop here. The Dutch Latch simply has one of the most commanding views of the island's east coast to be found, and the proof is apparent the moment you enter. It is probably best to come here during off-hours, for dessert or a snack, when the scenery is still glorious and the crowds and tour buses have thinned out.

VICTORIA

Victoria is accessible by ferryboat from Seattle, Anacortes and Port Angeles in Washington state, and from Tsawwassen Bay, Horseshoe Bay and Powell River on the mainland of British Columbia. From Seattle you can take a Stena Line ship (604) 388-7397 or (206) 624-6986 (or toll-free in the States (800) 962-5984 or Canada (800) 663-4495). Stena makes three direct crossings a day during the summer. During the fall and winter season there is only one sailing a day Monday through Thursday; on Friday and Saturday there are two. Each way is a 4 ½-hour trip. The passenger-only Victoria Clipper (206) 448-5000 is the fastest way to get there, 2½-hours each way.

As much as possible, this book avoids the big tourist draws, and without question, Victoria is a sprawling tourist center. But Victoria's charisma is hard to ignore. The famous Empress Hotel, Parliament buildings, Butchart Gardens, historical museums, wax museum, restaurants and British-style shops — all bordered by a thriving harbor and marina — make the city an attraction-seeker's Nirvana. And especially in summer, it gets very crowded, and that is hardly romantic. But this traditional English town can be wonderful, particularly off-season. It may even make you feel lustfully regal.

◆ Hotel/Bed & Breakfast Kissing ◆

ABIGAIL'S, Victoria
906 McClure Street
(604) 388-5363
Moderate to Very Expensive

Call for reservations and directions.

A brief retreat into the past seems to give the heart a rest from the stresses and strains of modern times. There are many ways to experience the pace of days gone by. One way is to travel the mountains, where civilization hasn't taken root; another is to sojourn to Abigail's and slip into dreamy, sophisticated comfort. This is a dazzling example of the country-inn experience and one of the finest accommodations in Victoria. Every nuance of comfort has been seen to and perfected. There is only one problem: is spending time in such sumptuous surroundings worth the financial splurge?

Abigail's is a classic Tudor mansion that has been renovated into a modern inn, finished in pastel shades of rose and green. Each room is designed with only one thing in mind — romance and guilt-free pampering. They have private spa tubs near wood-burning fireplaces, plush, richly colored carpeting, authentic washstands, winding wood staircases, thick goose-down comforters, and a generous, gracious breakfast. Of course, the more expensive rooms are the more luxurious, but they are really worth it. If you have a special occasion to celebrate, or can make up one, this would be an ideal place for the celebration.

◆ *Romantic Alternative:* **THE BEACONSFIELD**, 998 Humboldt Street (604) 384-4044 (Moderate to Expensive) is owned and managed by the same company that runs Abigail's, but unfortunately the prices here are high and the rooms somehow seem to miss the bill. As you would expect, the most expensive ones are the best, but even they could stand some attention and renovation. Some of the rooms do have spa tubs, sitting areas, loveseats, wood-burning fireplaces and unique touches like a canopied bathtub, stained glass windows and crystal chandeliers, which are all lovely but sound better than they actually turn out to be. Your best bet is to go for a room at Abigail's.

THE BEDFORD HOTEL, Victoria
1140 Government Street
(604) 384-6835
Expensive to Very Expensive

The hotel is three blocks north of the Empress Hotel on Government Street.

The Bedford is no ordinary large hotel. It has all the trappings of one, like room service, luggage handlers, a reception desk and yes, even elevators, but there the similarities stop and the heart-stirring differences begin. The rooms are striking and modern in tones of forest green and burgundy, and the bathrooms were built for two people to enjoy together. Some of the rooms have huge tiled shower stalls with two jets, others have spa tubs, still others have fireplaces, and then there are a few that have everything, including a view of the inner harbor. Added to all that is a deluxe complimentary breakfast and afternoon tea at the hotel's charming mezzanine-level restaurant. For an uptown getaway, The Bedford will fit your requirements and then some.

◆ *Romantic Warning:* The courtyard rooms have no views, and because they look directly across to the other units it is necessary to keep your shade pulled if you expect to have any privacy at all; this is not the best situation on a hot summer day.

THE EMPRESS HOTEL, Victoria
721 Government Street
(604) 384-8111
Expensive to Unbelievably Expensive

You can't miss it in the town center, near the marina on Government Street, between Humboldt and Belleville.

If you listen to those in the tourist trade, the words "Empress Hotel" and "Victoria" are usually uttered in the same breath. The classic, exalted Empress, with its elaborate, palatial elegance and pivotal location, has always epitomized this European-style city. But long-time patrons who have not been to Victoria in the last year or so will remember a somewhat haggard hotel that was begging for some physical attention. Well, over the past two years, Canadian Pacific Hotels & Resorts has spent $45 million bringing this place up to speed and if you were wondering how to spend that kind of money, this is an outstanding example of how to do it right.

Every detail has been seen to and the result is unequivocally spectacular.

There is the opulent **Crystal Tea Room** with its new $50,000 ceiling that must be seen to be appreciated; the formal, architecturally grand **Empress Dining Room**; the handsome, eminently comfortable **Dessert Lounge**; the charming **Garden Café**; and the unique **Benegal Restaurant**, casual only in comparison to the other dining spots here. All are stupendous. You won't be surprised to learn that these public areas feel like a museum complete with gawking tourists (among whom my husband and I were two). Still, you would be remiss if you didn't visit the Empress and stay for awhile over tea and crumpets or a sherry and dessert. As for making an overnight stay — the least expensive rooms are fairly small, though beautifully appointed, and as you move up in price the rooms definitely increase in size. Is it worth it? Well, if you can afford the steep tariffs, why not?

HOLLAND HOUSE, Victoria
595 Michigan Street
(604) 384-6644
Expensive to Very Expensive

Call for reservations and directions.

From outside there is little hint of the gorgeous, superior comfort that awaits you inside this continental-style inn. The bright interior is filled with the owner's striking modern art collection. A gourmet breakfast is served every morning in the quaint dining room, set with tables for two and framed by French doors that look out to the garden. And each unique guest suite is beautifully furnished, all with elegant baths and some with fireplaces. You will be in designer heaven in whichever room you find yourselves at Holland House.

◆ **Romantic Note:** Off-season there are special excursion packages with the Victoria Clipper from Seattle that include a stay at Holland House at bargain prices.

◆ ***Romantic Alternative:*** **JOAN BROWN'S BED & BREAKFAST,** 729 Pemberton Road, (604) 592-5929 (Inexpensive to

Moderate) is a vintage mansion that owner Ms. Brown has skillfully transformed into an attractive and endearing place to stay in Victoria. This stately home, has high beamed ceilings, seven fireplaces, stained glass windows, formal English gardens, finished-wood floors, the original wood staircase, comfortable furnishings and a mixture of room sizes (some with private bath). The larger rooms, particularly the one on the ground floor, are the most beautiful. If you relish an authentic English-style bed & breakfast stay, this place is a must.

OAK BAY GUEST HOUSE, Victoria

1052 Newport Avenue
(604) 598-3812
Inexpensive to Moderate

From Government Street turn east on Fort Street, then right on Oak Bay Avenue and right again on Newport Avenue.

Oak Bay Guest House has some very respectable neighbors. Across the street is the very ritzy Oak Bay Beach Hotel (one of the most expensive places to stay in Victoria), the Windsor Park Rose Garden, the Oak Bay Marina and the Victoria Golf Club. With great finesse the renovated Oak Bay Guest House successfully adds its own quiet gentility to this elite district.

The new innkeepers have surrounded the pale gray stucco exterior with colorful, beautifully landscaped gardens. Inside, everything has been improved. There are new carpets and wallpapers of gray, mauve and taupe, refinished woodwork, soft floral fabrics and newly added French doors and windows. The dining room has separate tables set for two and a large bay window that looks out to the garden. A large glass-enclosed sundeck furnished with wicker and high-backed chairs is a wonderful place for lounging and afternoon tea. Ten charming guestrooms, each with its own bath, fill the upstairs, but the best ones have fireplaces and bright sun-filled windows. All this plus reasonable rates and the ocean only a block away.

TIFFANY BAY, Saanichton
629 Senanas Drive (604) 652-4434
Moderate to Expensive

Call for reservations and directions. Saanichton is a suburb of Victoria.

From the moment we entered this waterfront estate we felt as if we had walked into a Hollywood movie set from the '20s. Our spacious suite had its own wood-burning fireplace, a spa tub placed next to a towering window with a breathtaking view of the scenery, and French doors that opened onto a balcony poised over the indoor, azure, window-enclosed swimming pool. A spiral staircase allowed easy access to this glamorous aquatic setting which was almost entirely glass enclosed and precisely heated. We literally could have played in the pool all day.

When we exited through the sliding glass doors that led from the pool to a large deck overlooking the forested hills of Saanich Inlet, we found a private cove just a step or two off the deck, and the inlet waters were warm enough for a secluded ocean dip. Now we wanted to stay here forever!

Every moment was sheer heaven. Even breakfast was fantastic — a Grand Marnier soufflé one day and crepes with fresh berries the next. This may not be Breakfast at Tiffany's, but it's probably the next best thing.

◆ *Romantic Alternative:* **PEGGY'S COVE BED & BREAKFAST**, 279 Coal Point Lane, Sidney, (604) 656-5656 is a few miles north of Tiffany's and offers a totally different yet thoroughly stunning romantic environment. It's not the rooms here that are the draw, though they're nice enough; it's the enormous hot tub. This idyllic spa is surrounded by Japanese lanterns and meticulously kept woodland, and it overlooks the spectacular waters of the Saanich Inlet. Outside one of the larger rooms, there's even a newly built Japanese waterfall that cascades over six tiers of immaculate gardens. Breakfast is a fabulous presentation of fresh fruits, granolas and your favorite egg dish or souffle.

◆ *Second Romantic Alternative:* **GREAT-SNORING-ON-SEA**, 10858 Madrona Drive, Sidney, (604) 656-9549, is a very appropriate name for this cliffside bed & breakfast, because if you can't sleep well here, you can't sleep well anywhere. Yet it isn't the guestrooms that are responsible for the state of tranquility you will achieve during your stay. The two guest suites, each with its own small bath, are nice but nothing special, though the room with the view of the water is the best. Probably the most important restful assistance comes from the built-in swimming pool, the wraparound deck with a large hot tub, and the stunning views of Saanich Inlet. And then there are the "surprises" that the innkeepers take a great deal of pride in creating for you. I have been asked not to tell you about these, but I promise they will make you feel pampered and spoiled.

◆ Restaurant Kissing ◆

THE CAPTAIN'S PALACE RESTAURANT, Victoria   ❤
309 Belleville Street
(604) 388-9191
Inexpensive to Expensive

Across the street from the ferry dock and to the left, you will see Heritage Village. Next to the Village is The Captain's Palace.

If you haven't already gotten your fill of Victoriana, venture into The Captain's Palace for an opulent turn-of-the-century experience of tea, dessert or a snack. The pomp and flourishes of the interior make an ideal setting for a quiet tête-à-tête or an evening sip of brandy. The lavish appointments that accompany a taste of sherry or an attentively served breakfast include stained glass windows, frescoed ceilings, stately marble and wood fireplaces, crystal chandeliers, antique furnishings and a sweeping stairway with a carved banister.

◆ *Romantic Warning:* The Captain's Palace is expensive and the food isn't quite up to the standards of some of the less-ornate dining establishments in town. That is why we recommend only an off-hour visit to enjoy the romantic setting. The warning, though, is about the bed & breakfast rooms. Located above the restaurant and in a building next door, these rooms could be wonderful if care and proper attention were given them, but at present they are second-rate and run-down.

THE GRAND CENTRAL CAFÉ, Victoria
555 Johnson Street
(604) 386-4747
Moderate

Between Wharf and Government on Johnson Street, enter through a small flower-clad alley.

Our lunch at the Grand Central Café was a festive, splendid affair. The flower-lined alley walkway was bright and fetching and the café is set far enough off the street to make it seem remote and hidden. Grand Central's outdoor patio was filled with more flowers, and there were umbrella tables. Inside, the brick-walled dining room, pale green ceiling, the terra-cotta floor, and the arched floor-to-ceiling windows that allow the sun to come streaming in — all combine for an appealing setting. The menu spanned continents and included dishes from Indonesia, Mexico, Italy, Spain and the American South. The peanut sauce over tender vegetables was rich and flavorful, and the pasta we ordered was good but a little disappointing given the way we felt about the surroundings. Nevertheless, we earnestly enjoyed every minute we spent here.

LAROUSSE, Victoria
1619 Store Street
(604) 386-3454
Expensive

On Store Street between Pandora and Fisgard.

Almost all of the innkeepers I talked to during my stay in Victoria told me that Larousse was *the* restaurant in town. I discovered they were right. This was one of the finest dining experiences I had in Victoria, and the style of the place was a match for the food. The ambience is subtle and refined, with European charm radiating from the soft multicolored walls of blue, lavender, gray, green and coral. The food is prepared with finesse, the freshest ingredients possible and a straightforward adherence to healthful cooking — that means low cholesterol. This is a place where self-indulgence won't affect your heart except for the better. There are memorable specialties every night: salmon mousse or fresh halibut complemented with a smooth, piquant sauce, vegetable side dishes that are as pretty as they are tasty, and desserts that are too good to pass up. A dinner at Larousse will be an unusual gourmet affair to remember.

LA PETITE COLOMBE, Victoria
604 Broughton (604) 383-3234
Moderate to Expensive

On Broughton between Government and Douglas Streets.

Restaurants don't get much sexier than this one. Besides truly exquisite French cuisine, the interior is sultry and lavish. The walls are a dark shade of eggplant, scarlet chairs are placed around a handful of linen-draped tables, and elegant sconces are suspended from arched mirrors that reflect a burnished light against this dramatic interior. There are only a handful of tables in the small dining room, which adds to the intimate ambience.

◆ Outdoor Kissing ◆

MOUNT DOUGLAS PARK, Victoria

From Highway 17, five miles north of downtown Victoria, exit to the east on Cordova Bay Road. Follow this road south to the park.

Minutes away from the center of Victoria is a 500-acre rain forest on the ocean's edge miles away from the tourists and the city. A walk down one of the many beach trails will bring you out to a winding stretch of shoreline. From here you can look across to the island-dotted Haro Strait. This area is suprisingly quiet and serene. Don't forget to bring a blanket and picnic provisions so you can spend a leisurely afternoon out here without interruption.

◆ ***Romantic Suggestion:*** After a day of losing yourselves in Mount Douglas Park, stop at **CORDOVA SEAVIEW INN**, 5109 Cordova Bay Road, Victoria, (604) 658-5227 (Moderate) and relax on the cliffside patio, where you'll have a bird's-eye view of the wild and peaceful landscape you were just romping through.

SOOKE HARBOUR HOUSE, Sooke

1528 Whiffen Spit Road
(604) 642-3421
Very Expensive to Unbelievably Expensive

Go west of Victoria on the Trans-Canada Highway until it intersects with Highway 14. Take Highway 14 to the town of Sooke (about 25 miles northwest of Victoria). North of town you will see signs for Sooke Harbour House. At Whiffen Spit Road, turn left and continue till the dead-end.

Sooke Harbour House has undergone an outstanding and fabulous renaissance. The restaurant remains stellar, and the menu preparations are, if possible, better and fresher than ever. The herb garden still supplies the seasonings, and an outdoor tank keeps the shellfish until it's prepared just for you. The dining room is located in a charming, two-story country house where windows facing the harbor let in warm, soothing sunlight.

As a bed & breakfast, Sooke Harbour House is a sensational lovers' getaway. There are exquisite guest suites in a building next door, and the rooms in the main house have also been completely refurbished. All are simply sensational. No detail has been overlooked in any of the rooms, and the views are captivating. Regardless of where you choose, you'll find yourselves in the lap of luxury. Each suite has a private spa tub or outdoor hot tub, fireplace, separate sitting area, vaulted ceiling, view of the water, wet bar, balcony or patio, king-size beds and beautiful furnishings. Sigh, this MUST be what heaven is like. These suites will be hard to leave, even for the delectable breakfast or lunch (both are included in the price of the room) that are served daily.

◆ *Romantic Suggestion:* For either a short morning hike or a rugged all-day jaunt, **EAST SOOKE REGIONAL PARK** provides 3,500 acres of wilderness with phenomenal views and trails winding through beautiful beaches and pristine forest.

HOUSE ON THE BAY, Sooke
7954 West Coast Road
(604) 642-6534
Moderate

Call for reservations and directions.

For the price and comfort it offers, House on the Bay is a great alternative to the expensive Sooke Harbour House. It is located on three acres and rests atop a steep cliff with an expansive view of the Strait of Juan de Fuca and the mountains on the Olympic Peninsula across the water. The two-level home has cathedral ceilings of cedar, and lofty windows that make the hallowed outside an integral part of the inside.

The two suites are spacious and incredibly comfortable. Each one has a private entrance and patio with a far-reaching view, individually designed Japanese-style soak tubs built for two (sans spa jets), kimonos for after your bath, wide showers, queen-size beds, armchairs and Ikebana-style fresh floral arrangements throughout the year. The decor is best described as Rustic '50s, which isn't elegant, but you'll be so relaxed you won't notice. The breakfast is equal to the accommodations and is served in your room: your choice of juice, any egg-style you want, homemade croissants, cereals and fresh coffee. House on the Bay offers a total package, with all the trimmings you'll need. You also have the restaurant at Sooke Harbour House only 10 minutes away and the beach only a short hike from your front door.

MARGISON TEA HOUSE, Sooke
6605 Sooke Road
(604) 642-3620
Inexpensive

In the town of Sooke, off Highway 14, 25 miles northwest of Victoria. As you enter Sooke on Highway 14, watch for a sign indicating the driveway to the house.

A tablecloth draped over a table set with fine china, steaming aromatic tea in silver service, finger sandwiches and cakes on a silver caddy—all are essential to the English tradition of afternoon tea. While passing through this amorous countryside, take the time to do what the natives do and sip some tea, have a bite of cake and nibble a finger sandwich or two.

There is no better place to do all this than Margison Tea House. This enchanting, delightfully arrayed home-turned-restaurant is just off the main road in the seaside town of Sooke. The garden supplies all of the fare, including the floral arrangements. The emphasis here is on superior quality, service and cozy surroundings. Everything is meticulously displayed and proudly served. You may never be the same after holding hands in such an engaging setting during this important time of day.

◆ *Romantic Note:* A self-contained cottage set in the expansive garden here is available for a devoted twosome. This adorable bungalow and immaculate landscape is a comfortable private haven where you'll have everything you need including a great morning breakfast.

MALAHAT FARM, Sooke
R.R. 2 Anderson Road
(604) 642-6868
Inexpensive to Moderate

Directly off Highway 14, a short drive north from the town of Sooke.

Set back from the road, with little else around but 45 acres of forested meadows and farmland, a soaring hawk overhead and abundant serenity, this country home offers gracious hospitality and comfort to its guests. Malahat Farm is a rustic hideaway where hours float by while you renew your relationship with each other and the earth. The rooms are large and cozy, with fireplaces and views of the surrounding peaceful landscape. Breakfast is a hearty undertaking with homemade breads and jams, farm-fresh eggs and fresh honey. This place doesn't offer luxurious accommodations, only pure and simple relaxation and beauty.

CHINA BEACH & FRENCH BEACH
Follow Highway 14 past Sooke. You will see a sign 10 miles down the road for French Beach. Further along on Highway 14, one mile past the Jordan River, look for the China Beach sign. China Beach is accessible by a 15-minute walk through rain forest. French Beach is reached by a short tree-lined path down to the shore.

These two beaches are separated by a few miles but share similar settings and a rugged character. You can ramble through young, replanted forests or formidable groves of ancient trees, or along white sandy beaches that stretch forever in either direction. Sure-footedness is a prerequisite, though, for you will occasionally have to make your way over projecting headlands of rocky coast and woods. At either location, you can bask in solitary freedom while being lulled by the water's music on the shore. Beautiful views are abundant along this relatively undiscovered coastline just a short jaunt from the bustling town of Victoria.

POINT NO POINT RESORT, Sooke
West Coast Road
(604) 646-2020
Inexpensive to Moderate

Forty miles northwest of Victoria, on Highway 14, watch the west side of the road for a small sign for Point No Point.

Despite the name, there is nothing resort-like about Point No Point. The rustic cabins are set amidst pure rugged beauty and seem eons away from civilization. Regardless of the weather or time of year, the isolation of this place spells romance. In addition to the simple rustic cabins with fireplaces, there are rooms in an adjacent building that rests on the edge of a cliff overlooking a crashing granite shoreline. Trails with foliage-covered stone archways lead down to a nearby inlet and small beach. The 11 cabins have large picture windows revealing an unobstructed view of the ocean and Olympic mountains. Even on a cloud-veiled day, Point No Point is a magical place softened by the muted colors of ocean and forest.

THE GULF ISLANDS

Saturna, Mayne, Pender, Galiano, Salt Spring, Gabriola, Hornby, Denman, Quadra and Cortez Islands are accessible via ferryboat from Tsawwassen Bay just south of Vancouver and from several locations on Vancouver Island. For ferry information in Vancouver call (604) 669-1211; in Seattle (206) 624-6663; or in Victoria (604) 386-3431. Depending on the season and during most weekends, reservations and advance payment may be necessary to assure your place on the ferry. Departure times are limited, so be sure to make your travel plans with this in mind.

The Gulf Islands lie nestled between Vancouver Island and mainland British Columbia, scattered like a heavenly constellation up and down the coast. There are over 300 forested isles, whose populations vary from a few hundred to several thousand. The Gulf Islands resemble the San Juan Islands of Washington state, and they are all places of transcendent splendor and solitude.

A handful of the Gulf Islands are accessible by ferryboat, and each of these has what's required to give you a hassle-free, all-absorbing time away from everything except nature and each other. Whichever island you choose, you will be certain to find oceanfront parks with sweeping views of the other islands, bed & breakfasts set on hilltops or hidden in the woods, unique restaurants where "leisurely" is a way of life, and miles of meandering paved roads that lead to island privacy. The only things to distract your attention will be the out-of-this-world scenery and the eyes of the person you love.

OCEANWOOD, Mayne Island
C-2 Leighton Lane
(604) 539-5074
Moderate to Expensive

Call for reservations and very detailed directions on how to get here. This island can be tricky and the map almost impossible to follow.

After our first evening here I couldn't wait to write this entry. However, ahem, other things kept me occupied so that all I could do was take some quick notes while my husband and I indulged ourselves in this unbelievably romantic location.

Oceanwood is a renovated Tudor home with an assortment of outstanding rooms, cozy sitting areas, and a 30-seat country-gourmet restaurant. Our spacious suite was flawless, exquisitely designed for cherished time together. There were French doors that opened onto our own patio overlooking a forested inlet of the island, the spa tub was positioned next to a glowing marble-hearthed fireplace, a flower-patterned sofa was placed in front of the crackling embers, and the firm, ultra-cushy bed and down comforter were splendidly comfortable. It was sheer bliss. All the rooms we saw at Oceanwood were just as beautifully done as ours, but the rooms with fireplaces, private terraces and patios, views of the water and en-suite spa tubs are, without question, the best.

Breakfast and dinner are served in the idyllic dining room, framed on one side by a brick fireplace and on the other by a glass-enclosed solarium. The continental dinner menu is impressive, and the kitchen's ability soars when the going gets tough. Potato leek soup, stuffed leg of lamb, fresh halibut in parchment, and strawberry cheesecake with hazelnut crust are some of the selections you might find on the menu. Breakfast is served to guests only and is a scrumptious presentation of fresh-baked muffins and breads, pancakes with fresh berries, and freshly squeezed juices.

My recommendation is that you pack your bags right now, because there's no better time to take advantage of what Oceanwood has to offer.

FERNHILL LODGE, Mayne Island

Box 140
(604) 539-2544
Moderate

Call for reservations and directions.

This place is a food-lovers' must. Besides being a comfortable and meticulously maintained bed & breakfast, Fernhill Lodge also offers a totally exotic dining experience. It's hard to imagine that a feast like this could possibly be found in the countryside of a remote island — or anywhere else, for that matter. Julia Child would be envious of the chef's nightly creations served in the lodge's somewhat austere, rustic dining room.

On any given night between May and October you will find three different four-course theme dinners based on a particular time in history. The Renaissance period is evoked with slivers of smoked eel in fruit sauces, a garden-picked salad with quail eggs, barbecued lamb in sweet and sour citrus sauce, and sweet and spicy pear pie. The Roman motif is highlighted with dates fried in honey and olive oil and sprinkled with pepper, barbecued pigeon with mustard and nut sauce, lentil and chestnut potage, and cheese and honey balls. Fabulous!

When dinner is over you can retire to your room, which overlooks the extensive garden and hillside and is decorated in one of four period themes. An overnight adventure at Fernhill Lodge will be a rapturous one for your hearts and your tastebuds.

LA BERENGERIE RESTAURANT, Galiano Island
R.R. 1 Montague Harbour Road
(604) 539-5392
Inexpensive to Moderate

From the ferry landing turn left and follow the signs to Montague Harbour along Sturdies Bay Road, merging left onto Georgeson Bay Road and then Montague Harbour Road, where you will see a sign for the restaurant.

Galiano Island is long and peaceful, with acres upon acres of vigorous forest and gorgeous shoreline. The main reason to come here, it would seem, is to hide from the world for a period of time, filling yourselves up on being close and enjoying nature and silence the likes of which you've never heard before. But surprise! Tucked away in the woods you will find an authentic French country restaurant that caters to knowledgeable palates and eager stomachs. La Berengerie is a wonderfully rustic restaurant. It has only 10 tables and the prix fixe menu is remarkable. Fresh tomato soup, stuffed chicken breast and blueberry cheesecake made for a delectable meal the night we were there.

TALL TREES, Galiano Island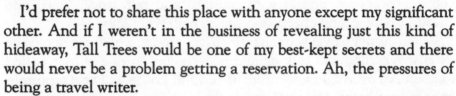
Montague Harbour Park Road
(604) 539-5365
Moderate

Call for reservations and directions.

I'd prefer not to share this place with anyone except my significant other. And if I weren't in the business of revealing just this kind of hideaway, Tall Trees would be one of my best-kept secrets and there would never be a problem getting a reservation. Ah, the pressures of being a travel writer.

Well, I could lie and say it isn't a remarkable, tranquil spot to spend time with your beloved. And there are ways to avoid explaining such details as the cloistered private entrance or the madrona-framed deck that overlooks the breathtaking harbor, forested cliffs and sparkling water, or the glass-enclosed bedroom with the same scintillating view. After all, you may not find Tall Trees as delciously cozy and attractive as I did and then it wouldn't really be fibbing after all, now would it? But then how would I get around describing the spacious bathroom with a fabulous soaking tub that cradles two quite nicely, the plush terrycloth robes, or the freshly prepared breakfast served on a silver tea trolley in your room every morning? I almost forgot about the afternoon tea service set out in your suite, complete with cookies and chocolates.

I guess it's best to tell the truth, but for a minute or two I admit the temptation was almost too great. Tall Trees is a romantic revelation.

WOODSTONE COUNTRY INN, Galiano Island

R.R. 1 Georgeson Bay Road
(604) 539-2022
Inexpensive to Moderate

From the ferry landing turn left and follow Sturdies Bay Road to Georgeson Bay Road. Turn left to the inn.

Set amidst a landscape of forested farmland, Woodstone Country Inn is a newly built hideaway nestled in the hills of Galiano Island. My only hesitation about this beautifully constructed inn is the location. Generally, when it comes to islands, I prefer shimmering water views. Well, a rural setting hardly inhibits kissing, and besides, there are 12 lovely rooms here, most with views of the forest or rolling valley, and 10 of the 12 have fireplaces and a handful have soaker tubs. Each unit is attractively furnished, though a bit plain, and each radiates a great deal of warmth. After only a few hours here, you will have achieved a maximum amount of relaxation and peace of mind.

There is a restaurant on the ground floor of Woodstone Country Inn. This charming country kitchen, scattered with wood tables covered in lace tablecloths, is immaculate and gracious. There's a serene view of the valley through floor-to-ceiling windows. A complimentary breakfast is served here to guests every morning, and at night a superb four-course dinner is presented by candlelight to the accompaniment of soft classical music. Broccoli apple soup served with homemade herb bread, oysters gratin, sole stuffed with salmon mousse in a grape cream sauce, and espresso cheesecake are some of the menu's glittering surprises. If you are on Galiano, don't miss this epicurean country dining spot.

CLIFFSIDE INN, North Pender Island

Armadale Road
(604) 629-6691
Moderate

From the Otter Bay ferry terminal follow all highway signs indicating

Hope Bay. At the Hope Bay dock, take Clam Bay Road for half a mile east to Armadale Road. Turn north and proceed 800 feet to Cliffside.

A requirement for any romantic holiday is to travel to an awe-inspiring place and, once you arrive, not to travel anywhere else for anything. This enables you to spend uninterrupted precious time in relaxation and cuddling. Ferrying to Pender Island will grant you awesome scenery and seclusion, and Cliffside Inn guarantees all the cozy amenities.

This bed & breakfast inn straddles a bluff above three acres of concealed oceanfront with wondrous panoramas that take in Mount Baker and Navy Channel. All the rooms have private decks, sun-filled windows, private patios, fireplaces and titillating glimpses of the gardens and ocean. An outside deck also has a hot tub that you can reserve for private steamy interludes. The cozy restaurant is a glass-enclosed solarium that opens onto a wood deck with more of the same entrancing vistas. If weather permits, your meals will be served out here. From all reports, including our own experience, the kitchen here consistently prepares supremely fresh, delicious meals. Morning may bring fresh-made muffins, a smoked salmon omelet seasoned with herbs from the garden, and a homemade rhubarb raspberry compote topped with yogurt. Evening is an epicurean repast, lovingly served in the candlelit room. Fresh pumpernickel bread, oysters wrapped in back bacon, stuffed squash and fresh lamb cooked in red wine, mushrooms and herbs — all are knowingly prepared.

Every romantic requirement for staying together in undisturbed privacy, serenity and absolute pampered comfort will be met, in style, at Cliffside Inn.

HASTINGS HOUSE, Salt Spring Island

Box 1110, Ganges
(604) 537-2362
Expensive to Unbelievably Expensive

Take the ferryboat from any of the islands to Long Harbour. Follow the signs on Long Harbour Road to the town of Ganges and head west. Turn south on Robinson Road; watch for signs that direct you to the house.

Hastings House is a sparkling gem of a country inn, poised over Ganges Harbour and the rolling hills of Salt Spring Island. Everything about this place will tug at your heartstrings, imploring you to stay longer and luxuriate in the distinguished renovated buildings of this 30-acre seaside estate. Unfortunately, Hastings House will also pull at your pursestrings, even if you select one of their smaller rooms. And the strings may break altogether if you want a two-story suite with a classic stone fireplace, two bathrooms and personalized afternoon-tea service. Every morning before your full-course breakfast is served in the fireplace-warmed cottage dining room, a basket of fresh pastries and hot coffee are delivered to your door. As the Hastings House brochure aptly states: "Meticulous attention is given to character, courtesy, comfort, calm and cuisine." As one couple who stayed here told me, "Every time we kissed, someone wanted to come in and straighten up the room."

Hastings House is one of the most expensive, exclusive places to stay on the west coast of Canada. If the cost exceeds your holiday budget but you want a taste of this regal style of living, have dinner at their country restaurant, which serves sumptuous, tantalizing gourmet fare. Regrettably, there's a dress code; men *must* wear jackets. The management hasn't yet adapted to West Coast ways. They must think they're in Toronto or Montreal.

◆ *Romantic Option:* For those who prefer less pretentious, less dear accommodations while trysting on Salt Spring Island, **SOUTHDOWN FARM BED & BREAKFAST,** 1121 Beaver Point Road, Fulford Harbour, (604) 653-4322 (Moderate) is an exceptional alternative. There is only one private, sunlit cottage here set amongst pristine farmland, orchards, woods and ponds. It has a spa tub, woodstove, thick down comforter and a lovely interior. Breakfast is a wonderful occasion with farm-fresh eggs, juice and pastries, and will assuage your appetites until dinnertime.

BAY WINDOW RESTAURANT, Salt Spring Island
375 Baker Road
(604) 537-5651
Moderate

Call for information about seasonal hours, reservations and directions.

From the lace-covered windows at the rustic, tasteful Bay Window Restaurant, located in the time-worn lodge of Booth Bay Resort, you can observe the changing contours of Vancouver Island as the sun moves effortlessly through the sky. Dinner here is a perfect accompaniment to such a scintillating panorama. The menu is traditionally French, with such dishes as coq au vin, rack of lamb bearnaise, and fillet of sole meuniere. Everything here is cooked to perfection and even the Baked Alaska is a delight. After dinner, if it's low tide, you can walk along the shore and dig for clams and oysters, or if high tide brings the crystal-clear blue water closer in, you can take off your shoes and walk along the warm surf.

BEACHHOUSE BED & BREAKFAST, Salt Spring
Sunset Drive, Ganges
(604) 537-2879
Expensive

Call for reservations and directions.

Along the northwest shore of Salt Spring Island, far removed from the bustling villages of Ganges or Vesuvius, this enticing cottage is an idyllic retreat. Your self-contained cabin sits on an incline above its own private cove, and has bay windows through which you'll watch startling sunsets over the mountains of Vancouver Island. There are bathrobes to snuggle in while you rest on your deck watching the otters and seals frolic in the waves. Down comforter, feather pillows, petite kitchen and sitting room are all yours. Breakfast is a culinary event at the Beachhouse; one of the innkeepers was schooled at Cordon Bleu in Paris. Delicacies such as blueberry coffeecake, salmon quiche, fresh brioche, homemade sausages, and unique fruit drinks may be served to you in the morning.

◆ *Romantic Note:* There are two rooms in the main building here at Beachhouse that are small, have no view and share a bath. I would not recommend either of these. However, the innkeepers are planning some fairly wonderful-looking renovations (they let me peek at the floor plans) and if they work out, these suites would be every inch as desirable as the cabin. Only time will tell.

OLD FARMHOUSE BED & BREAKFAST, Salt Spring
1077 Northern Road, Ganges
(604) 537-4113
Inexpensive to Moderate

Call for reservations and directions.

The number of bed & breakfasts on Salt Spring Island has grown from 31 to 85 in little more than a year. This explosion means a lot of work for a travel writer and a lot of confusion for travelers about the quality of the accommodations. Sometimes having only a few choices is better than having too many. After exhaustive lip research I found the best this wonderful island oasis has to offer, and The Old Farmhouse is one of those discoveries.

Nestled among billowing trees, bountiful orchards and lush meadows, this revitalized turn-of-the-century farmhouse has everything you'll need for a sublime getaway. The 4 guestrooms are located in a separate building next to the main house. Each has its own entrance, private bath, separate balcony or patio overlooking the peaceful landscape, high dormers, down comforters, bright, cheerful fabrics and colors, and lots of space. Outside there is a picnic table in the orchard and plenty of sweet, fresh air. In the main dining room a gourmet country breakfast is meticulously served each day with selections like creme fraiche over kiwis and blueberries, homemade cinnamon buns and croissants, and eggs Florentine in a light pastry shell.

◆ *Romantic Alternative:* **CRANBERRY RIDGE BED & BREAKFAST**, 269 Donore Road, (604) 537-4854 (Moderate) is located near the town of Ganges, on a ridge with a mesmerizing view of the islands, inlets, and the imperial coastal mountains of the mainland. This home offers one of the most magnificent panoramas imaginable. The two guestrooms are located in the bottom section of the house and they are rather pretty and quite large, with wicker furniture, sitting areas, terrycloth robes and floor-to-ceiling sliding glass doors that look out on this stunning scenery. There's an expansive deck with a great hot tub for stargazing during late-night soaks. A couple of drawbacks I should mention: There are only half-baths in each room, with a shared bath down the hall; and when the shades are open to let in the view through beautiful glass doors, you'll feel rather exposed. Breakfast in the morning more than makes up for any of these considerations — and then there's that endless vista.

TRIBUNE BAY, Hornby Island

From Vancouver Island take the ferryboat from Buckley Bay to Denman Island. Cross Denman following the sign to the Hornby ferry. From the Hornby ferry dock follow Central Road to the small Coop Center and follow the signs a short distance to the bay.

A visit to Hornby Island is like a visit to Woodstock, New York, circa 1968. The dress, manner and conversations in the Coop Center, where most of the Island activity takes place, will make you feel that you've entered a time warp. (I'm young enough to remember this lifestyle and old enough to be startled when I see it still operating in full swing.) There are two rather good foodstands here that serve the most delicious vegetarian fare I've had in a long time, and a darn good espresso to boot. But none of that is a provocative reason to come to Hornby Island. Rather it is the gorgeous sandy beaches, crystal-clear blue water and gentle coves and bays that make this island a desirable destination.

Summertime has never felt this good in Southwestern, Canada. The soft sand under your feet, the surf warmed by the sun, and the forested backdrop of Tribune Bay are absolutely gorgeous.

WE-WAI-KAI CAMPGROUND, Quadra Island
Rebecca Spit
(604) 285-3111
Incredibly Inexpensive

From the ferry landing follow the signs to the ferry for Cortes Island or Heriot Bay. When you see the water, start looking for signs to Rebecca Spit. The campground is located on the spit.

I don't usually think of camping as being particularly romantic. It's not that I don't enjoy it, it's just that I don't think it's the best environment for intimate, tender moments. Kids running about, other campers too nearby, mosquitoes, hard ground, somewhat inaccessible showers, and my personal nemesis — outhouses — tend to keep the mood neighborly but not private. So when I tell you that Wa-Wai-Kai campground is one of the most beautiful and well-laid-out of any I've seen in the islands, you can be certain this must be one spectacular setting.

One group of campsites is located on the beach facing the calm inner bay, another is just above the shore surrounded by trees lining the upper bank, and yet another lies above this in the forested hills overlooking the water. Each one is beautifully maintained and spacious. Even the common facilities are decent. I wouldn't go so far as to say that your privacy is guaranteed, but your relationship with each other and nature will be greatly enhanced.

◆ *Romantic Note:* Just a few feet from the campground is **REBECCA SPIT PROVINCIAL PARK.** This rare parkland has remarkable vistas, short but wonderful trails, shoreline of the tranquil bay on one side and the open waters of the strait on the other. The contrast between the two, only a mere stone's throw apart, is stupendous. There are picnic tables here and a convenient parking area as well.

> *"A kiss is a lovely trick designed to stop speech when words become superfluous."*
>
> **Ingrid Bergman**

VANCOUVER AREA

VANCOUVER

From Seattle head north on Interstate 5 and cross the Canadian border. Follow Highway 99 into Vancouver via the Oak Street Bridge.

Vancouver has so much to offer and its geography is so beautiful that it's a stunning model of a big city done right. From Stanley Park and the sea wall to the historic-preservation district of Gastown, from the skyline encircling English Bay to the formal gardens and botanically magnificent conservatories, from the sophisticated architecture of downtown, the three mountains that border the city on the north and the island-flecked Strait of Georgia — all is romantic and all is fastidiously maintained.

Here the excitement of city life is manifested in miles of lights, steel-girded bridges and skyscrapers, yet the urban landscape also embraces snow-capped mountains, forested parks and salt-water beaches. The vibrant, varied surroundings will entice you to seek out the inexhaustible daytime sights and the hot nightlife action. Prepare yourselves for the time of your lives.

◆ *Romantic Note:* For more detailed travel guidance while in British Columbia, consult the visitor information centres scattered generously along most major roads and in most towns. The people here are so lovely, you should stop in just to say hello and get your first taste of Canadian hospitality. For Vancouver information, write to the **Vancouver Visitors Bureau**, #1625 -1055 West Georgia Street, P.O. Box 11142, Royal Centre, Vancouver V6E 4C8, or telephone (604) 682-2222.

◆ *Second Romantic Note:* Though there are several services you can call for a listing of bed & breakfast-type accommodations in the area, they're likely to net you a bed in someone's home and only a 50/50 chance of a comfortable arrangement. One of the more reliable bed & breakfast reservation services in Vancouver is the **Best Canadian Bed**

& Breakfast Network, (604) 738-7207. If you make clear to them your specific requirements, such as private bath, private entrance, city or country setting, you are likely to get what you want.

◆ Hotel/Bed & Breakfast Kissing ◆

BEACHSIDE BED & BREAKFAST, West Vancouver   💋
4208 Evergreen Avenue
(604) 922-7773
Inexpensive to Moderate
Call for reservations and directions.

I'm still not sure why there are so few bed & breakfasts in the Vancouver area; I've been told it has something to do with licensing problems. But I searched for the best among the few this city has to offer, and Beachside Bed & Breakfast is one of those finds.

It isn't often that I recommend a place solely for its location and view, but the waterfront setting of this home — in the very exclusive, very wealthy section of West Vancouver — is exceptional and makes up for some of the less than romantic details. The rooms here are just mediocre, with average comfort and a pleasant style. They're located on the lower floors of the main home without, sad to say, a share in the spectacular view. That's the down side. But the good news is that all the guests have access to the living and dining rooms which have floor-to-ceiling windows overlooking the water, the beachside hot tub, and an outdoor barbecue area that is perfect for nighttime bonfires. Breakfast is a noteworthy event enriched by the sound of the waves lapping against the shore.

BESSBOROUGH COTTAGE, West Vancouver

2587 Lawson Avenue
(604) 925-3085
Inexpensive

Call for reservations and directions.

From the moment we entered, we knew this charming cottage, nestled in a tranquil neighborhood of West Vancouver, would be an affectionate place for a not-so-out-of-town sojourn. We walked up the brick patio, surrounded by a slightly overgrown garden bursting with an array of colorful blooms, and saw a view of the bay in the distance. Here, insulated from the rest of the world, we could shake off our frazzled nerves and achieve serenity. The suite was exceptionally cozy yet roomy, with its own private entrance, furnished in white wicker and white linens. The bay window was covered in lace, and the cathedral ceiling had a sizable skylight which made the cottage very bright and cheerful. A generous breakfast is served either in the comfort of your room, on your personal patio, or in the family dining room. There is only one unit here, so if you're lucky enough to get a reservation you'll have a delightful place to stay.

HOTEL VANCOUVER — See Roof Restaurant (Restaurant Kissing)

LABURNUM COTTAGE, North Vancouver

1388 Terrace Avenue North
(604) 988-4877
Moderate

Call for reservations and directions.

If downtown Vancouver seems a bit too hectic for you overnight, then consider a stay in either North Vancouver or West Vancouver. Both of these affluent, sophisticated communities lie just north of the city at the foot of Grouse Mountain, Hollyburn Mountain and Mount Seymour. Both communities provide fabulous settings that are only minutes from the city. By far the finest bed & breakfast in North Vancouver is Laburnum Cottage. The name refers to the rustic cabin set amidst a lush English garden, haloed by forested parkland in back of the main house. The cabin is a very private, very attractive though somewhat small place to spend quiet moments. (Of course, where intimacy is concerned, small is not necessarily a problem.)

Inside the main house, on the second floor, are three bright, extremely comfortable, nice-size rooms, each with its own newly renovated bath, ultra-thick carpeting, and luxuriant down comforter and view of the garden. Though the rooms here are wonderful, there are no common areas that can be used by the guests, and the continental breakfast left much to be desired. Still, none of that signifigantly detracts from the comfort, privacy and tranquility you will find in any of the guest quarters at Laburnum Cottage.

LE MERIDIEN HOTEL — See Gerard Restaurant (Restaurant Kissing)

PAN PACIFIC VANCOUVER, Vancouver
999 Canada Place
(604) 662-8111
Expensive to Unbelievably Expensive

On the waterfront at the north end of the city, between Burrard and Howe Streets.

Achieving romance at the huge Pan Pacific Hotel in downtown Vancouver may at first seem impossible. The entire complex is more like a small city than anything else. There is a large shopping mall on the lower floors, and cruise ships dock along here as well. The gargantuan exterior and interior have an air of sterile impersonality. Nevertheless, this landmark building is an exceptionally stunning, professionally run, exciting place to stay, with superbly designed rooms that other hotels could learn from. All the units have stupendous views, canopied, firm beds, soft colors, and chic marble bathrooms. Of course the less expensive rooms (which are still fairly expensive) are rather small, and the rooms in the Unbelievably Expensive category are more spacious and luxurious. The health club is as up-to-date as they get, and the immense outdoor pool and sundeck are impressive. The Pan Pacific is still just a hotel, but with enough frills to make it a rare experience.

THE WEDGEWOOD HOTEL, Vancouver
845 Hornby Street
(604) 689-7777
Expensive to Unbelievably Expensive

On Hornby Street in downtown Vancouver, between Burrard and Howe.

Of all the gigantic formal hotels in downtown Vancouver, my favorite is the relatively petite Wedgewood. Its white French doors open onto an elegant lobby and an attractive, quiet lounge that has not been taken over by the serious business-suit crowd. The guest-rooms have separate sitting areas, which helps you feel that you're staying in an uptown apartment rather than a downtown hotel. There are fireplaces in many of the suites and all of them have foliage-draped decks that help alleviate the claustrophobia that high-rises tend to induce.

The Wedgewood dining room, **LIAISONS,** is one of the most graceful, demure places in Vancouver for an intimate lunch or dinner. In the winter you will be warmed by the glowing fireplace, in summer you will be cooled by the bright white and green tones of the decor, and throughout the year the well-prepared food will revitalize and please.

For a more lively luncheon or night on the town, the hotel's **BACCHUS RISTORANTE** will delight you with its truly casual elegance and robust Italian food. You have the option of dancing or just listening to the live band play Latin tunes, depending on your inclination and hips. This is not disco dancing by any stretch of the imagination, but I wouldn't call it Lambada either. An easy arm-in-arm samba or two-step will do just fine.

WEST END GUEST HOUSE, Vancouver
1362 Haro Street
(604) 681-2889
Inexpensive to Moderate

Located on Haro Street one block south of Robson Street, between Jervis and Broughton Streets.

Once you hear about West End Guest House, you won't be surprised if you have difficulty getting reservations there. It's practically the only professionally run bed & breakfast in town, and except for its overly bright exterior, everything about the place is wonderful and endearing, including its six-block proximity to Stanley Park. This electric-pink turn-of-the-century house is dwarfed by two large, modern apartment buildings on either side, in a neighborhood that is almost exclusively high-rises; it's a bit startling when you first see it.

The inside has a much gentler persona. It has been beautifully restored and decorated in an imaginative blend of practical and whimsical: striking blond-wood trim, high ceilings, crystal chandeliers, bay windows, soft down quilts, private, adorable bathrooms, and a breakfast area with individual wood tables. There are modern conveniences, like televisions and telephones, without the usual sterility. For a romantic change from the ritzy, skyscraper hotels, West End Guest House is a soothing alternative.

◆ **Romantic Option:** If West End Guest House is booked, the innkeepers there may direct you to **THE BARCLAY HOTEL**, 1348 Robson Street, (604) 688-8850 (Inexpensive to Moderate). This is not a bed & breakfast, nor is it exactly a hotel; it is more like a European inn, with appealing, quaint architecture on the outside and cozy, proper rooms on the inside — like those that face the busy streets of Paris or Brussels. Only you are here, on Robson Street, one of the most lively, fashionable shopping districts on the West Coast.

◆ Restaurant Kissing ◆

CAFFÉ DE MEDICI, Vancouver ◆◆◆
1025 Robson Street
(604) 669-9322
Moderate to Expensive

On Robson between Burrard and Thurlow.

Robson Street is a confluence of specialty shops, bakeries, cafés, bistros, superb restaurants and designer boutiques, traveling a half-mile course through downtown. Centered in one of the more swank clusters of shops, tucked away from the bustle of the street, is Caffé de Medici. This Northern Italian restaurant is artistically designed with colors of forest green and maroon, high arched ceilings, muraled walls and thick plush drapery. The polished, unmistakably romantic interior is matched by the rich, delicious entrees and flawless, genteel service. On Robson Street, where the choices for dining out seem endless, Caffé de Medici helps you narrow the field.

◆ *Romantic Option:* Caffé de Medici's next-door neighbor is a fabulous French restaurant, **LE MISTRAL**, 1025 Robson Street, (604) 687-1105 (Expensive to Very Expensive). Its stately, dramatic interior, with a handful of tables and a multitude of waitpersons, is an ultra-elegant atmosphere in which to spend an evening dining on sumptuous, classic French food.

CAPERS, West Vancouver
2496 Marine Drive (604) 925-3316
Inexpensive to Moderate

At 25th and West Marine Drive.

There is no way anyone could have convinced me that a restaurant located at the back of a health-food-oriented grocery store could be a suitable or desirable setting for a gourmet meal at almost any time of day. Well, seeing (and eating, with a kiss or two thrown in for good measure) is believing (though early morning, before the grocery opens, and dinnertime, after the grocery has closed for the evening, are definitely the most suitable times for intimate dining here.) The lovely, newly renovated interior — wood paneling, white tablecloths, forest green accents, large glass-enclosed deck with a view of the shore and English Bay, and soft classical music playing in the background — sets an appealing scene. The menu (not entirely vegetarian) is a whole-wheat, organic, al dente dream come true. Everything we sampled was excellent; even the vegetable pie with miso cashew gravy was light and perfectly cooked, and the service was professional and friendly. I know this kind of cuisine is not for everyone, and a grocery store backdrop is not the best, but it is definitely for you if you admire wholesome cooking served with an elegant flare.

◆ *Romantic Alternative:* If **CHESA SEAFOOD RESTAU-RANT**, West Vancouver, 2168 Marine Drive, (604) 922-3312 (Inexpensive), with its contemporary rose-colored, bright interior were located two blocks closer to the water or a half mile higher up the hill to the north, you would have to make a reservation months in advance. As it is, the restaurant's stark storefront location on well-traveled Marine Drive keeps the crowds in abeyance. Location aside, our meal here was so heavenly, and the overly generous serving of salmon, lightly smoked and charbroiled, so superior that if it wasn't my job to try other establishments, I would keep on returning here. With all due respect, Chesa is not a romantically endearing spot, but at these prices and with this kind of food quality, your appetites will be well taken care of.

◆ *Second Romantic Alternative:* Sometimes the view alone is enough to establish a place's romantic dining credentials. When the sunset casts vibrant color over the sky as the two of you share your deepest thoughts, some authentically intimate moments can occur. In places such as this, more often than not, the view is really all there is, and the food is given only a superficial amount of attention from the management. Believe it or not, **SALMON HOUSE ON THE HILL**, 2229 Folkestone Way,

(604) 926-3212 (Moderate to Expensive) has both a stupendous view and really excellent food. Reserve a table near the window, order the savory alderwood-broiled salmon, and then sit back and let the evening drift by your ringside seat on the world.

DELILAH'S, Vancouver
1906 Haro Street
(604) 687-3424
Moderate

On Haro near Gilford Street.

Of all the dining experiences that are available in Vancouver — and there are a bounty of premium choices — I would encourage you to make reservations at this absolutely unique restaurant. Everything here is an exuberant blend of fantasy, elegance and eccentricity. For some tastes, this restaurant's personality may be a bit overwhelming; it is not the most subtle of dining spots, but it is unquestionably the most entertaining and winsome.

Delilah's is located in the basement of the old Buchanan Hotel, in the heart of the West End, just a few blocks from Stanley Park. A small pink and yellow neon sign marks the entrance. Inside you'll find a dramatic mural-painted ceiling, plush red-velvet scalloped banquettes, floral carpeting, and chandelier lighting. There is also outdoor seating in the garden. The menu is a fill-in-the-blank prix fixe affair that you hand over to the waitperson when you have made your selections. You can check off oysters pan-fried in cornmeal served with a papaya relish, oven-roasted pork loin sauteed with Southern Comfort and dried cherries, or sake-marinated salmon served with a very hot vinaigrette. The service is efficient and the food superb. With its fine setting and cuisine, dinner at Delilah's makes for a flamboyant evening.

LA BROCHETTE — See Grouse Mountain (Outdoor Kissing)

LE GAVROCHE, Vancouver
1616 Alberni Street
(604) 685-3924
Expensive to Very Expensive

On Alberni Street between Cardero and Bidwell Streets.

Perhaps one of the most traditionally romantic dining atmospheres in the entire Vancouver area is to be found at Le Gavroche. The restaurant is lodged in a renovated Victorian home with a view of the bay from cozy nooks and alcoves that used to be the dining and living rooms. You enter on the ground level and walk up a carpeted staircase to the dining area, which has all the appropriate polished detailing. In style, everything here is essentially French. The service is nearly regal yet really quite friendly. Though ultra-formal dining is not usually my idea of an affectionate undertaking, there is something very romantic about this place. After all, formal doesn't have to be stuffy. It's all in the management's disposition and your frame of mind. Of course, the food here is a gastronomic triumph, with every dish a complete masterpiece. *Bon appetit et bon amour.*

GERARD RESTAURANT, Vancouver
Meridien Hotel
845 Burrard Street
(604) 682-5511
Expensive to Very Expensive

Located in the Meridien Hotel in downtown Vancouver, on Burrard Street between Smythe and Robson.

Gerard Restaurant is more popularly known as Gerard's, but that is as abbreviated as it gets — you would never think of calling it Gerry's. This very posh and very dignified dining room is located in the very extravagant **MERIDIEN HOTEL**. Be aware that dinner here is not in any way, shape or form a laid-back dining event. Quite the contrary; it is one of those stately, glamorous affairs, where dressing to the nines is a must so you can have dinner by seven. (I have since been informed by management that the dress requirements have been relaxed. It seems they have come to terms with their Northwest location. Men now do not have to wear jackets, but I still wouldn't call this place casual.) The renowned menu is either à la carte or prix fixe, and if a bit of posh continental dining is your way of celebrating together, Gerard's is de rigueur for the occasion. The lounge at Gerard Restaurant is also a handsome room, mahogany-paneled with a glowing fireplace that features intimate corners where privacy is almost always guaranteed.

The Meridien Hotel features a truly lavish Sunday brunch — considered to be one of the finest in town — at their attractive **CAFÉ FLEURI**. It is worth the visit, if only to experience their Chocoholic Buffet. It is decadent and wantonly sinful, but worth every mouth-watering calorie and the weeks of repentance that follow.

◆ *Romantic Option:* For a less expensive but truly adept French restaurant, venture into the **CHEF & THE CARPENTER** on 1745 Robson Street, Vancouver, (604) 687-2700 (Moderate). This quaint, intimate dining room and the enterprising cuisine will guarantee you a gourmet-romantic meal. After dinner, if the mood seems right, go enjoy a snifter of brandy at the lounge at Gerard's.

PICCOLO MONDO RESTAURANT, Vancouver
850 Thurlow Street
(604) 688-1633
Moderate to Expensive

On Thurlow Street just south of Robson.

A strong recommendation from the innkeepers at West End Guest House (and they thoroughly understand my criteria) prompted us to make reservations at Piccolo Mondo. In addition to our being in the mood for Italian cuisine, they had further tempted me by describing the ambience as luxurious and comfortable. A peek through the windows left no doubt about the ambience recommendation. The interior was indeed handsome, with wood paneling and rich tan and sable colors. Northern Italian is the specialty here, and the pasta combinations are a blend of the freshest herbs and cheeses with rich silky sauces. The portions aren't the biggest, but each bite will be a pleasure.

THE PROW RESTAURANT, Vancouver
999 Canada Place
(604) 684-1339
Moderate to Expensive

Canada Place is at the intersection of Howe and Cordova Streets, on the eastern coastline of downtown, where the cruise ships dock beside the Pan Pacific Hotel.

Dinner at this establishment will be an indelible romantic episode in your lives. How can it fail? The dining room overlooks the Burrard Inlet, set off by mountains, glittering city lights and imperious ships forging their way through the water. The interior is dressed in pastel peaches and greens, and the tables have room to spare between them. Add to all this a menu as outstanding as the view is heart-throbbing and you have a restaurant that transcends its touristy location. The fish seem to have jumped from the water to the kitchen, and these dishes are adorned with oyster mushrooms and light cream sauces that have been carefully prepared. The desserts are bountiful—and well, there's that view again. From the setting to the cuisine, this location is satisfying all the way around.

◆ *Romantic Note:* If The Prow Restaurant is crowded, you can always relax awhile next door in **CASCADES LOUNGE** in the **PAN PACIFIC HOTEL**, (800) 663-1515. This immense, airy, echoing bar shares the same astonishing view as the restaurant, through arresting floor-to-ceiling windows. Not the prettiest of interiors, nor even vaguely intimate, but with each other and what's outside you'll do just fine until your table at The Prow opens up.

ROOF RESTAURANT and LOUNGE, Vancouver

Hotel Vancouver
900 West Georgia Street
(604) 684-3131
Very Expensive

On Georgia Street at Hornby.

This is not the most beautiful restaurant in Vancouver, and it is hardly the place to come for renowned French cuisine, but I still think it's a distinctive setting for celebrating a special occasion. This is obvious from the moment you enter the room. The Roof is located on top of the Hotel Vancouver, with a sweeping view of the city from the glass-enclosed dining room. Up here on cloud nine, with the city lights twinkling below, you can do some honest cheek-to-cheek, arm-in-arm dancing while the band plays on and on. The melodious tones of a three-piece band, with a somewhat Latin flavor, are heard seven nights a week. If you ever wanted to dance the light fantastic, this is the place to do it, in style, with some supreme atmosphere and service. If the price of dinner seems a bit steep, or if you prefer to dine somewhere else, The Roof's lounge area is separated from the dining room and band by only a rise in elevation, and is totally accessible to the dance floor.

◆ *Romantic Suggestion:* THE HOTEL VANCOUVER, 900 West Georgia Street, (604) 684-3131 (Very Expensive) is as venerable a hotel as you will find in downtown Vancouver. The formidable stone exterior, replete with gargoyles and old-English style, contrasts with the bright, crystal-chandeliered, red-carpeted, lush interior. The rooms have been nicely redone in a formal, business-executive style, slick and professional, with all the amenities in place. Plus there is a large, outdoor glass-enclosed pool. For an exclusive celebration in a grand setting in downtown Vancouver, this is the place.

THE TEAHOUSE RESTAURANT, Vancouver
Stanley Park at Ferguson Point
(604) 669-3281
Moderate

From the north end of the park, turn west off Highway 99 and follow Stanley Park Drive along the park's western side. Follow the signs to the teahouse.

This restaurant is a truly extraordinary kissing place. And it's hard to believe that such a major tourist attraction can also be one of the more beautiful places to dine in British Columbia. A large part of the sparkle comes from the location: The Teahouse rests in the middle of a sloping lawn overlooking English Bay and, on the horizon, Vancouver Island. The building itself is dazzling, half of it a pastel-colored country home, the other half a glass-enclosed atrium. Here you can watch the sun gently tuck itself into the ocean for a peaceful night's rest — that is, if you have reservations. Everyone, including the busloads of tourists, knows about The Teahouse Restaurant. The restaurant serves fairly standard Canadian-French cuisine that is a tad too standard and generally over-sauced, but not all the time. The seafood, baked egg dishes, and meats, when prepared au natural, can be tasty, so order carefully. But that view! Sigh. Your hearts and eyes will be thankful for a long time to come.

◆ *Romantic Note:* **STANLEY PARK** is a spectacular oasis of thick forest, green hilly lawns and lakes, with paved trails weaving through its 1,000 acres of cloistered parkland. The park is almost like an island, projecting as it does into the water, with English Bay on one side and Burrard Inlet on the other. From the **SEA WALL PROMENADE** that wraps around the park, to the zoo, aquarium, picnic areas galore, the lengthy shoreline at Sunset Beach, vistas and more vistas, restaurants and lakes, Stanley Park is a refuge from the cityscape only moments away. The only problem is that it's so extraordinary, everyone loves it and that doesn't leave much room for privacy. But the surroundings are so welcoming, you can forgive the busloads of camera-clicking tourists and find yourselves a corner to call your own — at least for a while.

◆ Outdoor Kissing ◆

DEEP COVE, North Vancouver

Take Highway 1 through North Vancouver, over the Second Narrows Bridge. Follow the signs for the Mount Seymour Parkway exit heading east. Stay on the Parkway until you come to Deep Cove Road, then turn north. The road dead-ends at Deep Cove.

A mountain-circled marina, a single rural-style main street relatively untouched by commercialization, and a small forested park with wooden stairs leading down to the water: this is Deep Cove. The small village of Deep Cove looks north to Mount Seymour and west to an arcade of mountains separated from the town by a vast body of water called Indian Arm. Deep Cove is so close to Vancouver that it's easy to engineer a trip out here. The area is a quiet celebration both of nature's ability to create astonishing, enduring scenery and of people's ability to leave well enough alone.

◆ *Romantic Warning:* As of this writing there was some fairly major construction going on in the heart of Deep Cove. It is hard to say how this will affect the area, but locals seem to have a positive feeling about it, a rather unique reaction given the scale of development.

GROUSE MOUNTAIN, West Vancouver ◆◆◆◆
CYPRESS PROVINCIAL PARK, West Vancouver
MOUNT SEYMOUR PROVINCIAL PARK, North Vancouver

These three mountains areas are accessible from Highway 1 and Highway 1A/ 99. To get to Mount Seymour Provincial Park, follow the signs from Highway 1 heading east from the Lion's Gate Bridge. Cypress Bowl Road in West Vancouver takes you to Cypress Provincial Park. Capilano Road in West Vancouver leads to Grouse Mountain.

One extraordinary aspect of Vancouver is that in its very own backyard there are three separate mountains high enough above sea level to be active ski areas, and they are only about 30 minutes from the city (45 minutes if you take your time or get lost). It is quite feasible to spend an invigorating day on any of these mountains hiking, lake-swimming (depending on the season), gazing out over the stupendous views or skiing, and still have more than enough time to get back to the city and dress up for a candlelit, sumptuous dinner in a place like **LA BROCHETTE**, 52 Alexander Street, (604) 684-0631 (Moderate), in Gastown, where freshly roasted quail, duck and lamb are standard items on the hearty French menu. The interior is all dark wood paneling and dim lighting, and there is an intimate lounge on the lower level with cozy seating around a stone fireplace appropriately well-stoked all evening long.

◆ *Romantic Warning:* Both park areas are well-known, but Grouse Mountain tends to be the most touristy of the group. This is only a sunny-weekend warning. At evening and during the week there are enough private corners up here for everyone.

◆ *Romantic Suggestion:* On a moonlit winter's eve, the more adventurous couple may consider doing the above scenario in reverse. After an early dinner in the city, gather your cross-country ski equipment, toss it in the car and drive up to Cypress Provincial Park. Stride over the sparkling white snow until the park lights shut off at 11:00 P.M.

JAPANESE GARDENS, Vancouver

In Vancouver, off Northwest Marine Drive, on the grounds of the University of British Columbia. There is a fee to get into the garden.

"Mysterious" and "captivating" are words not often associated with a garden, yet they succinctly describe the imagery and impact of the Japanese Gardens. Coaxed from the earth by skilled artisans, this botanical presentation is creative and authentic, with delicately sculpted shrubbery crowned by specially pruned trees. A quiet afternoon spent here will be like visiting another country, without the trouble of obtaining passports.

LIGHTHOUSE PARK, West Vancouver　　

From Highway 1/99 in West Vancouver, take the 21st Street exit to Marine Drive. Follow the signs on Marine Drive to Lighthouse Park.

At the southwestern tip of West Vancouver there's a peninsula called Lighthouse Park. It is a small, water-bound fragment of granite hanging on to the mainland. From the parking area, the shores of Georgia Strait or the clifftops of the parkland are both only a brisk 15-minute walk over trails through rocky forest. Along any of the trails you can inhale the freshness of sea air mingling with the scent of sturdy fir and spruce trees. At trail's end, you'll get a far-reaching view on a clear day. On a cloudy day, Lighthouse Park obligingly resembles the kind of dense forest that exists deep in the distant mountains of the Canadian Rockies, enabling you to feel far away from city life. The two of you will scarcely remember how close civilization really is.

◆ **Romantic Alternative:** After heading back east on Marine Drive from Lighthouse Park and passing through the town of West Vancouver, look for a waterfront park called **AMBLESIDE** just west of Lion's Gate Bridge. The long, winding sidewalk that outlines the park is bordered on one side by a stone sea wall with marvelous views of the water and city, and on the other by grass and playgrounds. This is a much smaller, less crowded version of the sea wall in Stanley Park, and a definite romantic option if crowds are something you like to avoid.

LYNN CANYON SUSPENSION BRIDGE,　　
North Vancouver

Take Highway 1 east from the Lions Gate Bridge and follow the signs to Lynn Canyon Park.

I'm not so much afraid of heights as I am of falling. I have no problem with how far off the ground I am, so long as I feel secure and "grounded." There is no way to have such a feeling on a suspension bridge, and my anxiety intensified every time anyone else on the bridge moved an inch. Regardless of the number of people I saw pass back and forth effortlessly across the Lynn Canyon bridge, I found myself frozen, incapable of moving. What a predicament. I needed to check out the Lynn Canyon area as a possible entry, and the only way to get there was to walk over this ridiculous bridge.

The material I'd read described a suspension bridge across a rocky, forested gorge where a waterfall and river etched its way through the canyon floor below. On the other side of the bridge there were supposed to be trails that led to a boulder-strewn brook with freshwater soaking pools. You could cross over the rocks and find a refreshing niche all to yourselves. Plus this was not a tourist attraction like the Capilano suspension bridge just a few miles to the west of here — no crowds, no entrance fee, no tourist shops, and when school was in session, a certain amount of privacy. I *had* to get across that bridge!

Sometimes I'm amazed at what I'm willing to do to make this book complete — but let's just say I made it across and it was exactly as I had pictured it to be — totally beautiful. (I also deserved every kiss my husband showered me with once I calmed down.)

MARINE DRIVE, West Vancouver

Marine Drive follows the southern shoreline of West Vancouver. Heading north over the Lion's Gate Bridge, turn west onto Marine Drive.

Marine Drive follows, at water's edge, one of the most fabulous residential neighborhoods in the Vancouver area. Summertime graces this road with perfect views of the city and Vancouver Island. During the fall, overcast rainy days make this sinuous road more reclusive, emphasizing its dark, rocky cliffs and the thick, moist foliage that veils the houses along the way.

Besides being scenic and conducive to sitting close (if you don't have bucket seats), Marine Drive has an added attraction: there are several satellite roads off the Drive that lead northward and connect with two alternative routes to Whistler—Cypress Access Road through Cypress Provincial Park, and Capilano Road over Grouse Mountain. Let the beauty of the drive lead you wherever it compels you to go.

"The real value of love is the increased general vitality it produces."

Paul Valery

WHISTLER

WHISTLER VILLAGE

From Vancouver, heading north over the Lions Gate Bridge, follow the signs for Highway 1 west, which will split off to Highway 99 north to Whistler. Two miles after you enter the town of Whistler on Highway 99, turn right into the entrance for Whistler Village.

The first serious snowfall of the year beckons skiers to the slopes of Whistler and Blackcomb Mountains, world renowned for their stupendous cross-country and downhill skiing. The world-class resort facilities of Whistler Village and the surrounding area are unsurpassed anywhere in the entire Northwest and Canadian Southwest. This is an international developer's dream come true. Designer homes, mountainside condominium complexes, chateau-style hotels and an assortment of inns, bed & breakfasts and lodges can accommodate thousands of visitors a day. Perhaps the only drawback to this mountainous holiday-mecca is that the town of Whistler is growing so fast; with so much building taking place, the area has some elements of urban sprawl —convenient for skiing, and highly social, but not necessarily intriguing or charming. You needn't be too concerned with any of this, though, since the suggestions that follow will help you find the romantic sparkle and secret solitude that still abound in this part of Canada.

Aside from skiing, Whistler's raison d'être is the enjoyment of every outdoor recreational activity you can imagine: kayaking, canoeing, wind surfing, white-water rafting, hiking, mountain biking and golfing. If you like high-paced fun and a party atmosphere amid purple mountain majesty, Whistler delivers in the slickest, most impressive way possible.

◆ *Romantic Note:* During the summer there is glacier skiing available at the very top of Blackcomb Mountain. It's not the mile-long runs of the winter season, but then again, in winter you can't wear your bathing suit on the slopes.

◆ Hotel/Bed & Breakfast Kissing ◆

CHALET LUISE PENSION, Whistler   ●●
7461 Ambassador Crescent
(604) 932-4187
Inexpensive to Moderate

About one mile north of Whistler Village, turn right on Nancy Greene Drive and then right again on Ambassador Crescent. Go two blocks to the pension.

Whistler has several pensions that cater to those who want a more reclusive, less hectic residence than those in the heart of the Village or in a condominium complex. Almost all of these Swiss- or German-style, professionally run bed & breakfasts provide a homey environment and a hearty meal first thing in the morning just before the lifts open. Chalet Luise is just such a place and has a little bit of everything for those couples who want to be close to the mile-long mountain runs: quaint, exceptionally neat rooms (some a bit on the small side) with views and balconies, an outdoor whirlpool and a fireside lounge where breakfast is served. Individual tables are placed around the room and allow for a private morning repast of creative juice combinations, waffles, cereals, breads and jams. Plus there all the extra comforts and crisp clean detailing you would expect from a European-style bed & breakfast. Chalet Luise is only moments away from the slopes and cross-country ski runs, so once you arrive you may never need to use the car again during your winter stay.

◆ ***Romantic Option:*** Another impressive bed & breakfast is **HAUS HEIDI**, 7115 Nesters Road, (604) 932-3113 (Inexpensive to Moderate), set far enough away from intense Whistler Village to make it seem like a snow-clad island getaway. The interior is filled with handcrafted pine furnishings, plush, thick carpeting, European comforters, private baths, and a fireplace lounge area. Outside there is a wraparound deck with a steaming hot tub overlooking the exquisite alpine scenery. Breakfast is served around a large table and is a lavish presentation that that will leave you well prepared to tackle the slopes.

THE GABLES, Whistler Village
Sea-To-Sky Accommodations
(604) 932-4184
Moderate to Unbelievably Expensive

Two miles after you enter the town of Whistler on Highway 99, turn into the entrance for Whistler Village. Follow the road straight past the Village, and turn right where it dead-ends. The road curves around, heading toward the Wizard Express ski lift. You will see The Gables on the west side of the road, just before the lift.

Besides excellent ski runs and the latest in express chair lifts, Whistler is filled with condos of every size, shape and price. From the heart of the Village to the base of the gondola that ascends Whistler Mountain and even further out on the back roads, there are more than enough accommodations to suit the tastes and budgets of the hordes of winter-sports enthusiasts. The one thing you may find lacking is a place to soothe the muscles and the heart after a day of tackling the slopes.

The Gables is a small, elegant development just a two-minute walk from the Village and right across the street from the Wizard Express. In spite of this easy access, the units are surprisingly sedate and beautifully appointed, a far cry from the typical units in the area. In each apartment there is a small entry hall that nicely handles wet clothing and snow-laden boots. The living room is then entered through glass-paned French doors. All the units have fireplaces and fully equipped kitchens, and the bathrooms have spa tubs. In each unit the cozy loft bedroom overlooks the capacious living room. You can even choose whether your apartment will have a staggering view of the mountain or a soothing view of the rushing creek at the back of the property. All in all, The Gables' proximity to everything and the inviting quality of the rooms make it a fetching place to escape after a day's mountainous pursuits.

POWDERHORN, Whistler

Sea-To-Sky Accommodations
(604) 932-4184
Moderate to Unbelievably Expensive

Call for reservations and directions.

From the outside, given the highly stylized developments we passed on the way through town and the village to get here, we found Powderhorn disappointing. Its exterior was an uninviting mix of black steel and rose-colored cement that made it look like a rather average apartment high-rise. The single elevator and sterile hallways confirmed that impression. But once we turned the key on our unit, we were shocked: could this be the same building? Everything was picture perfect. The interior was bright and sunny with expansive windows, comfortable furnishings, large kitchen and a huge amount of space. Actually our unit was designed for a group of 6 or more, but we didn't miss those other bodies. If we had come with a group, though, we could still have accommodated our need for privacy. The master bedroom was in a separate wing just off the living room. It had a huge bathroom with a large spa tub and lofty windows. Outside on the roof another spa tub was available for everyone. Who says you can judge a book by its cover? (Except this book, of course.)

TIMBERLINE LODGE, Whistler

4122 Village Green
(800) 663-5474
Expensive

Turn into Whistler Village and follow the signs to Timberline Lodge.

My friend Julie, who loves romantic ski-weekends, asked me to find a cozy, adorable accommodation for her and her husband somewhere in the heart of Whistler Village. She felt strongly that half the experience of Whistler was the evening excitement of the town after the slopes were closed. I felt strongly that the Village had everything you could want for apres-skiing except romance. But far be it from me to decline a challenge, so I searched through every inn, lodge and hotel the Village had to offer and found Timberline Lodge. The place is an oasis of alpine comfort, with fireplaces, four-poster beds, terraces, wet bars, and spa tubs in each room. All the rooms are so unique, you'll need to request a detailed list to figure out which one will exactly meet your needs, but each is assured to satisfy the wishes of two skiers' hearts.

◆ *Romantic Option:* If keeping your feet on the ground in the Village is what the two of you prefer for a dining experience, consider an evening at **MYRTLE'S RESTAURANT**, 4122 Village Green, (604) 932-5211 (Expensive), in Timberline Lodge. Here the elegant French Colonial atmosphere, superior service and exceptional cuisine make every meal a formal romantic treat.

TYAX MOUNTAIN LAKE RESORT, Gold Bridge
Tyaughton Lake Road
(604) 238-2221
Moderate

North of Vancouver on Highway 99, drive through Whistler and Pemberton to the town of Gold Bridge. From the main road in Gold Bridge follow the signs to the resort.

An alpine meadow at the heart of the Canadian Rockies, a crystal clear lake, mountain goats roaming the hillside and eagles soaring overhead — this is the stuff of a romantic escape. Include in that picture an imposing log building enclosing 28 elegant, authentically countrified suites, private cabins, an outdoor hot tub and all the outdoor and indoor adventures you can imagine, and you have described Tyax Resort. It's all there, along with three delectable, formal meals that are graciously served in the main lodge every day. The bread is baked in a huge stone oven and the freshest ingredients imaginable are deftly combined to satisfy the most discriminating of tastes.

Depending on the package you choose and the time of year you visit, the following are available to assure your outdoor entertainment: snowshoes, skates, toboggans, mountain bikes, ice-fishing equipment, snowmobiles, horseback riding, wind surfing, river rafting, heli-hiking, fishing tours, floatplane fishing, sleigh rides, canoeing, cross-country skiing, tennis and hayrides. For limitless romantic adventure, absolute privacy and breathtaking surroundings, this unique lodge is a short 110 miles north of Vancouver and relatively unknown to most Canadians and Americans.

◆ Restaurant Kissing ◆

CHRISTINE'S, Whistler
On Blackcomb Mountain
(604) 932-2775
Moderate to Expensive

Take the Wizard Express near Chateau Whistler and then transfer to the Solar Coaster and go up to the Rendezvous building where you will find the restaurant.

It's a shame this specialty dinner excursion, which takes place on top of the world, is really most idyllic during the summer. But Whistler's early sunset (about 4:00 P.M. during the height of winter season) makes this dining and viewing event mostly a summer fling. It is when the snow has melted (except for the perennial glacier patch at Blackcomb's summit) and sunset seems to linger forever across the face of the mountains that this unbelievable dinner and ride are possible and you learn what a feast in heaven must be like. The restaurant is open for lunch during the winter and summer (the patio barbecue is a thrilling experience), though there is something about dinner and sunset that is wildly romantic.

At the top of Blackcomb Mountain, Christine's awaits you with an impressive five-course, prix fixe dinner. As good as the food is, it is still only a minor part of your transcendent evening up here. It will take awhile for your eyes to adjust to the magnitude of the view from this dining location. To call this dinner-spectacle the apex of romance is an understatement, but until you venture up here and find out for yourselves, "apex" will have to do.

LES DEUX GROS, Whistler
1200 Alta Lake Road
(604) 932-4611
Moderate to Expensive

As you enter the town of Whistler, look on the east side of the road for Alta Lake Road. The restaurant is immediately up the hill on your left.

Two of Whistler's most respected chefs joined forces last year and opened one of the most exceptional restaurants in the area. Located two miles south of Whistler Village, this newly built country hideaway sits on a forested bluff overlooking the woods and mountain. The timber exterior blends fittingly with the area. Inside, the casual elegance of wood-beamed cathedral ceilings, floor-to-ceiling windows, cascading floral draperies and forest green and scarlet colors throughout blends perfectly with the sumptuous courses the kitchen ingeniously prepares. Classically French, your meal will be fantastic. There is also an outdoor patio for sultry summer dining.

RIMROCK CAFÉ AND OYSTER BAR, Whistler
2021 Whistler Road
(604) 932-5565
Moderate

After you enter the town of Whistler, look for the Highland Lodge just south of the gondola, at the base of Whistler Mountain, on the east side of the road. The restaurant is on the second story.

New construction rarely has an ambience of rustic charm. Even when a brand new place is tastefully done, it tends to look modern, not quaint. An exception to that rule is the restaurant at Highland Lodge, unromantically named Rimrock Café. Its two stone fireplaces fill the room with a blushing glow against the wood-paneled walls, the tables and floors. There is outdoor seating on the umbrella-covered patio during warm summer days. When it comes to the food, however, the spectacle is on your plate. The freshest of fish are bonded nicely with light sauces and served with tender vegetables, all flawlessly prepared and kindly served. After a madcap day of skiing or hiking, or a lazy afternoon communing with nature, this is a handsome place to have dinner. Unfortunately, it is also very popular and usually full (reservations are a must, sometimes a week in advance), and the nearby lounge has a live band playing first-rate rock n' roll. The music can be a bit loud and the volume of conversation increases to compete with the tunes, but between the food, setting and music, you will have a delightful evening.

◆ Outdoor Kissing ◆

BRANDYWINE FALLS

Take Highway 99 north to Whistler. A few miles before Whistler, you will see signs directing you to the falls.

A brisk 10-minute walk through lush forest will bring you to a feat of natural construction that deserves a standing ovation. At the end of your jaunt, pine trees open out onto a cliff from which you look across to the top of Brandywine Falls. The water drops down a tube-like canyon into the river, which cuts through a valley of interlacing mountains and meadows. During the summer you can climb down to the rocky ledges under the falls and, side by side, sit under the surging waters and feel the spray cool the sun's heat on your faces.

HIGHWAY 99

From Vancouver, cross into West Vancouver via Highway 1 north over the Second Narrows Bridge, or via Highway 1/99 over the Lion's Gate Bridge. Follow the signs to Squamish and Whistler. Depending on the road conditions, this is about a 1½-hour drive; of course, winter driving conditions can be hazardous.

There is nothing quite like rock, forest, snowcapped peaks and water all converging to stimulate the senses. The combination of perilously dropping cliffs, cerulean glacial flow, dramatic waterfalls and uninterrupted, fragrant pinery forms the best of all outdoor worlds. The drive along Highway 99, nicknamed the Sea-To-Sky Highway, is so gorgeous that you'll actually be relieved when a curve takes you away from the view and lets you get your mind back on driving. But since that doesn't happen very often during the first half of your trip, so be sure to agree beforehand about who's going to drive, or else take turns. Both of you should get a chance to gawk at the wonder that constitutes the 90 miles of curvaceous highway from Vancouver to Whistler.

MEAGER CREEK HOT SPRINGS, Pemberton

Take Highway 99 north past Whistler to the town of Pemberton. Follow the signs to Pemberton Meadows. Approximately 15 miles up the road toward Pemberton Meadows you will see a sign for the Coast Mountain Outdoor School. At this point, turn right onto Meager Main Line. Stay on this somewhat treacherous logging road for a bumpy 27 miles. At the sign for 27 miles, turn left. After you pass an area of felled timber, parking is a short distance ahead.

There are only a few kissing places in this book that are a pain to reach. A pain refers to a drive that is either long, boring, unattractive or a combination of all three, and road conditions that will eat your car alive. The drive to Meager Hot Springs is one of the trial-by-fire kind of drives, because a good deal of the trip is on eroded, active logging roads. If you have an all-terrain vehicle or a car that can take it, don't let any of that stop you. The hot dip that awaits you is unforgettable.

Once you arrive at the parking lot, a short footpath takes you into a maze of subterranean-heated pools and streams. A steamy mist rises lazily from the ground, extending to the rocky perimeters of the springs, and then disappears into the crisp-cool air above. As you bask together in the warm, soothing water, your attention will be drawn to the towering features beyond. Or if a vapory fog envelopes you, it will be easy to imagine that you are relaxing in a tropical climate behind an ethereal veil of privacy. Hot-tubbing at the health club was never like this! And talk about private — chances are you will have the entire place to yourselves.

◆ **Romantic Note:** Because these hot springs are not well-marked, and because this is an active logging road, call the Forest Service at (604) 898-9671 before starting your journey and obtain up-to-date information. Also be aware that nightfall or snow can create dangerous driving conditions.

SHANNON FALLS

North of Vancouver on Highway 99, about halfway to Whistler on the east side of the road. Look for signs that identify Shannon Falls.

Highway turnoff sites are both practical places to stop for momentary respites from the road and great ways to review where you've just been or where you're heading. You don't have to hike anywhere, the big-screen viewing begins the instant you stop. The turnoff to Shannon Falls is a turnoff-lover's view extravaganza.

Immediately after you pull off the main road into the parking area and silence the engine, you'll hear the thunder of a huge waterfall plummeting straight down the face of the mountain. One would expect to find such a spectacle at the end of a long, arduous trail and not in the middle of a rest area, but here it is nevertheless.

Before you leave Vancouver to start your trek up the mountain, be sure to pack a picnic to enjoy at the base of this lofty shower. Then you can take full advantage of this very accessible scenic paradise.

*"Love is better than spectacles
to make everything seem great."*
Sir P. Sidney

SUNSHINE COAST

GIBSON TO POWELL RIVER

The Sunshine Coast is accessible only by ferryboat from the Horseshoe Bay Ferry Terminal just past West Vancouver on Highway 99. The 40-minute ferry ride takes you through the mountain-ringed waters of Georgia Strait to Langdale. Here is where the Sunshine Coast starts.

It may seem odd that a part of the gray, rainy Canadian Southwest is referred to as "sunshine," yet once you travel this section of the world, you'll find no more applicable term. The Sunshine Coast provides all the wonderful rugged sights and sounds you could want, and some other getaway opportunities you didn't think existed. Regardless of weather conditions, even on a misty foggy morning, the Sunshine Coast is beautiful.

The Sunshine Coast is geographically unique. You'll feel as though you've stumbled accidentally onto a remote, lengthy peninsula or a long skinny island, and yet it is neither. This section of Canada, beginning at Gibson's ferry dock and ending at Powell River, is indeed part of the mainland, but because it's bordered on the north, south and west by water and on the east by mountains, it is accessible only by ferry. And even though the ferry from Horseshoe Bay, northwest of Vancouver, may seem packed, particularly on a summer day, and you may have to wait awhile to board it, the other cars will seem to disappear as you head north along the coast. It is unlikely you will have a sense of crowds again until you return to the mainland.

◆ *Romantic Warning:* The accommodations and most of the restaurants along the Sunshine Coast are best described as mediocre and are not even vaguely romantic. This is almost exclusively RV, camping and boating heaven. There are plenty of places to stay and eat, but they are not of the same caliber as those found on any of the Canadian islands or up on Whistler. Come here to enjoy the isolation and the incredible scenery available to the two of you at every turn.

◆ *Romantic Suggestion:* Before you start your travels north, you may want to make your plans together over a snack or meal at **MARINER'S RESTAURANT**, 399 Gibson, (604) 886-2334 (Moderate to Expensive) in the town of Gibson, a few miles north of the Langdale ferry dock. The small, rustic restaurant sits on a bluff overlooking the water. The visual splendor of the mountain-framed Strait will be a shining accompaniment to your meal.

CASSIDY'S, Gibson   ❥

Cassidy Road
(604) 886-7222
Inexpensive

From Highway 101 heading north, look for the Lower Road sign and turn left and then immediately veer to the right. A mile down the road, turn left at Gulf Road and then right onto Cassidy.

I would love to give this place a 4-lips rating. We were pampered and comfortable during our entire stay here. Breakfast was an outstanding array of freshly picked berries, a luscious cheese souffle, homemade huckleberry muffins, carrot coconut bread, and jams presented on English bone china. We were attentively served in the glass-enclosed solarium, where a wicker table and high-backed wicker chairs were framed by lush plants. On the sundeck there was a huge spa tub that overlooked the diverse, well-tended garden, tall fir trees and the sparkling waters of the Strait in the distance. Upon our departure we were even given a jar of the innkeeper's own blackberry jam.

It was all marvelous—except for the room, which was very small, and the bathroom, which was down the hall. Cassidy's is an authentic bed & breakfast where you literally share the home with the owners. It can feel a bit awkward if you're not accustomed to this style of accommodation. However, on the Sunshine Coast you will be hard put to do much better.

COUNTRY COTTAGE BED & BREAKFAST
Robert's Creek
(604) 885-7448
Inexpensive

Call for reservations and exact directions. The entire premises are strictly non-smoking.

Just up the street from Creek House (see next entry) is a perfect country alternative to almost any accommodation on the Sunshine Coast. It is one of the few professionally run bed & breakfasts around here and it is assuredly a place that is concerned with the needs of its guests. Still, there are only two rustic rooms available, and really only one that is truly conducive to intimacy — the cabin adjacent to the main house. It is comfortable and secluded and very much for the couple who likes to be away from everything and everyone.

Breakfast is served in the kitchen to the sound of the wood-burning stove crackling in the background. The sheep, hen house and rambling rose gardens can be part of your morning stroll as you sip coffee and wait for your farm-fresh breakfast to be served. After your hearty morning meal, the rest of the day can be spent lounging or searching out the area's adventures.

CREEK HOUSE, Robert's Creek
1041 Robert's Creek Road
(604) 885-9321
Expensive

Ten miles north of the Langdale ferry dock on Highway 101, you will find the turnoff for the town of Robert's Creek. Creek House restaurant is in the tiny town, across from the general store and post office.

French country-kitchen dining has a romantic flair all its own, due in part to the blend of elegance and rural-comforts. At Creek House, the relaxed, cordial ambience of a simply adorned dining room heated by a stone fireplace, and the supreme gourmet French cuisine are more than any two hearts can endure without succumbing to romantic urges.

◆ *Romantic Suggestion:* After dinner, take a walk or drive to **Robert's Creek Park** and behold a sunset that will complete a gratifying day.

BELLA BEACH MOTEL AND
THE WHARF RESTAURANT, Sechelt
R.R. 1 Bella Beach
(604) 885-7191
Inexpensive to Moderate

Twenty-five miles north of the ferry dock at Langdale, just south of Sechelt off Highway 101, on the east side of the road.

As I've mentioned, there isn't much in the way of romantic accommodations on the Sunshine Coast, unless you bring your own tent and stay in one of the many forested campgrounds lining the beaches and bays. But if roughing it isn't your idea of romance, Bella Beach Motel is one of your better options. Its large, comfortable, plain rooms face the vast ocean, with Vancouver Island looming in the distance. One drawback is that the main road lies between the motel and the water. Still, the view will engage you for hours and the traffic is never all that heavy, so the highway doesn't get in the way as much as you'd think.

The beach across the road and the accessibility to the entire coast make this a worthwhile place to use as a home base while you explore the area. You'll also be pleased that right next to Bella Beach is **THE WHARF RESTAURANT.** Breakfast and lunch are reasonably priced, the food is well prepared and the ambience cozy and attractive.

SECRET COVE

Follow Highway 101 ten miles past Sechelt to Secret Cove. The highway will turn into an unpaved road, which ends at a parking area. From the parking lot, a short hike will take you out to the cove.

This is is one of the coast's dozens of spectacular and isolated watery enclaves. After meandering a short distance through rain forest, you will be exposed to a view that is provocative in any weather. A sunny day reveals an entirely private inlet, etched from the finest assortment of rocky, jagged coastal formations. In the overcast opaqueness of a fall/winter day, you may imagine an English seaside underneath the clouds. Why not bring along some scones and a thermos filled with tea to snack on while you enjoy this haven. If by chance you hear some strange sounds emanating from the water or islands, don't be surprised. You've probably just happened upon a group of playful sea lions or otters frolicking in the afternoon sun or the evening tides.

◆ *Romantic Suggestion:* There are really only two dining options in this section of the Sunshine Coast: one is **LORD JIM'S**, Ole's Cove Road, (604) 885-7038 (Moderate to Expensive), and the other is **JOLLY ROGER INN**, Secret Cove, (206) 885-7184 (Moderate). Both of these restaurants are attached to relatively time-worn accommodations. Jolly Roger's restaurant definitely isn't romantic, though the view of the cove is beautiful and the food bland but fresh. Lord Jim's country elegant dining room attains high scores in the "trying" category: bay windows draped in green floral fabric, tables neatly covered in matching linens, and a view of the rocky crevasses lining Sechelt Inlet. It is all exceedingly pretty. The food is good but not great. I think the kitchen is straining to do what it does, and the service was unfriendly. Perhaps a breakfast or lunch here is the best idea, when everything — including the menu — is a bit more relaxed.

SKOOKUMCHUCK NARROWS, Egmont

Drive north from Gibson on Highway 101 about 60 miles, following the signs to the ferryboat at Earl's Cove. Just before reaching the dock, you will see signs for Egmont and the Narrows. Turn east and follow the road to the parking area. A quarter-mile hike will take you out to the Narrows.

The Canadian Southwest and the Pacific Northwest are filled with more than enough natural wonders to impress the most jaded world traveler. Skookumchuck Narrows is one of the more intriguing phenomena. The enormous energy that passes through this place is so moving (figuratively and literally), that indescribable feelings are triggered. The trail to the Narrows has abundant foliage — ground carpeted in autumn-colored leaves, and trees wrapped in leis of moss. As you make your way out to the tip of the peninsula, you'll approach Sechelt Inlet on the east side. You can stand almost at the edge of the rock-bordered gateway to this body of water. Through this tiny portal, at high or low tide, the rush of water is so intense that the land actually shakes beneath your feet. This is the time and place when, without even kissing or touching, you can really feel the earth move.

FERRYBOAT RIDE FROM EARL'S COVE TO SALTERY BAY

From the ferry dock at Langdale, follow the signs on Highway 101 to Earl's Cove at the northern end of the highway. Be sure to check the schedule for ferry crossings from Earl's Cove.

If you don't have a chance to become acquainted with the Sunshine Coast from your own or a chartered boat, then the ferry crossing from Earl's Cove to Saltery Bay is a must. The passage affords a rare opportunity to partake of the marine enchantment this area is famous for. There is an array of snow-capped mountains that frames your tour through the Jervis Inlet. The forested, rocky promontories jutting into the water are magnificent. Depending on the season, you may see whales as the ferry makes its way around and through this watery highway. This is one of the orcas' homes during the late winter and early spring, and they can perform at the most unexpected times of day.

"Come live with me and be my love, and we will all the pleasures prove, that hills and valleys, dales and fields, or woods or steep mountain yields."

Christopher Marlowe

WASHINGTON STATE

◆ Olympic Peninsula ◆

WILCOX HOUSE, Seabeck
2390 Tekiu Road
(206) 830-4492
Moderate

Call for directions and reservations.

A friend insisted that I check out Wilcox House. He promised it would make a perfect entry in this book. Unfortunately, his recommendation came just after the last edition of *The Best Places To Kiss* went to press. I decided to make Wilcox House my first destination for the new updated edition, and it's good thing I did, because it turned out to be one of the premier places to kiss on the Peninisula.

Last June I called for reservations and whisked my husband away to spend a quiet evening in the country. What we found exceeded our wildest imagination. Once we got off the ferry and passed Bremerton, we drove through 14 miles of towering evergreens and rolling countryside. As we reached the turnoff for the house, the road took a steep turn down to the water and we passed under a dramatic log-and-stone archway. In front of us there appeared an enormous, copper-roofed mansion, with terra-cotta tiles, resting on a forested bluff with views of Hood Canal and the Olympics.

The 10,000-square-foot interior is a renovated masterpiece (a bit on the eclectic side) that cost over $300,000 to create. Each room has been diligently brought back to life, from the copper-framed fireplaces, walnut wood paneling, scarlet wool carpeting and wood parquet floors, to the 600 new window panes. This place has to be seen to be believed! The two comfortable guest suites have views of the sweeping lawn, the gardens, mountain peaks and water; one has a spa tub, the other a private deck. There is also a built-in swimming pool in the backyard. Breakfast is a remarkable presentation of fresh fruits and waffles with homemade apple and blueberry syrups and apple and blueberry butters, served in the glass-enclosed dining room with more of the same impressive views.

◆ *Romantic Must:* The innkeepers at Wilcox House serve a formal four-course dinner on weekends which is available to guests as well as those not staying overnight. This is a meal you will thoroughly appreciate. Your salad will include 20 different greens and edible flowers, and you'll have freshly baked herb bread and creatively prepared vegetables, among other savory delights.

PORT TOWNSEND

From Seattle take the Winslow ferry to Bainbridge Island and follow the signs north to the Hood Canal Bridge. Take Highway 104 north to Highway 20 directly into Port Townsend.

Port Townsend, a small town at the extreme northeast corner of the Olympic Peninsula, was originally settled in the 1800s. The Victorian homes perched on a bluff overlooking the waterfront, and the parks, shops and restaurants of the town project an aura of charm and tranquility. The authentic restoration of period architecture is this town's trademark. A favorite weekend getaway for Seattleites escaping hectic urban life, especially in the summer, Port Townsend is cozy and slow-paced all year long. A walk around the waterfront district and the bluffs above it will give you outstanding views of the Olympics and the island-dotted Sound.

THE CABIN, Port Townsend
839 North Jacob Miller Road
(206) 385-5571
Inexpensive

Call for reservations and directions.

The Cabin is a very small, rustic cedar home that doesn't look like much from the outside, but the ultra-secluded location and the pioneer motif of the interior design make it really quite cozy (except for the rustic bathroom which is not the best). Plus the place is stocked with all the necessities of romance, including a tiny kitchen where fresh-baked delectables are delivered daily. You are invited to use the innkeepers' designer deck which has an extensive view over the Strait to Vancouver Island, and there is a fire pit outside for late-night bonfires. The real reason to come to The Cabin is for the peace and quiet, because the only sounds you'll hear during your stay are the breezes rustling in the trees, the waves lapping the shore, and the occasional horn of a tug or ship as it passes by on a cloudy morning.

JAMES HOUSE BED & BREAKFAST, Port Townsend

1238 Washington Street
(206) 385-1238
Inexpensive to Moderate

Take Highway 20 off Highway 101 to get to Port Townsend, where Highway 20 then becomes Sims Way. Before you enter the main part of town, look on your left for Washington Street which branches off and heads up a hill overlooking the waterfront.

James House has undergone some much-needed refurbishment by the new innkeepers who are infatuated with this venerable inn and are turning it back into the showplace it used to be. This handsome building — filled with fine, recovered and refinished period pieces, intricate handcrafted wood moldings, capacious, unique rooms — is as Victorian as they get in Port Townsend, and that's saying quite a bit. There are 12 rooms scattered throughout a labyrinth of hallways, parlors, bathrooms, and suites. There are lots of bay windows, fireplaces, white linens, views of the bay and mountains, and cozy alcoves designed for snuggling. A private cottage set in the well-tended garden is also available.

OLD CONSULATE INN, Port Townsend
313 Walker
(206) 385-6753
Inexpensive to Moderate

Take Highway 20 off Highway 101 to get to Port Townsend, where Highway 20 then becomes Sims Way. Before you enter the main part of town, look on your left for Washington Street which branches off and heads up a hill overlooking the waterfront. Follow Washington Street for about three blocks to Walker Street.

If you're smitten with the idea of pampering yourselves in an atmosphere of days gone by, with the modern addition of pleasing creature comforts, then Old Consulate Inn is exactly right for you. This gracious inn has a music room with an antique organ and grand piano, a fireplace-warmed study, a reading nook in the front parlor, a billiards/games room in the newly finished basement and a handsome wood-framed breakfast area. Elegant period antiques abound but never run to excess. At the top of the grand oak staircase you'll find 8 spacious private rooms, each with its own bath. There are sitting alcoves, turret lookouts, canopied king-size beds and expansive views of the waterfront. They are all such wonderful retreats that you'll want to leave only for breakfast.

The morning meal is a gastronomic fantasy come true. The inn proudly serves its own blend of designer coffee along with five full courses — fresh fruits, liqueur cakes, pastries, egg bakes, homemade granolas, and sherry or an appropriate liqueur.

RAVENSCROFT INN, Port Townsend
533 Quincy Street
(206) 385-2784
Inexpensive to Moderate

On Quincy Street between Clay and Franklin.

I've often heard that the best way to judge the overall quality of a hotel, inn or bed & breakfast is to look at the least expensive rooms in the house. If these units are nearly as splendid and comfortable as the more expensive ones, then you are assured of a sensational place with a management that really cares about its guests. Such is the case at Ravenscroft Inn.

Every guestroom in this newly constructed redwood inn is supreme. Many of the suites have French doors that open onto a balcony with views of the bay and mountains, some have spacious sitting areas and fireplaces. And every room has immaculate, attractive baths, plush comfort, unlimited privacy and room to spare. The open kitchen borders the dining area where a stone fireplace warms the room as your breakfast is served. Classical music accompanies such creations as a frappe of frozen berries, bananas and yogurt, a layered egg dish of tomatoes, onions and spinach, Cointreau-drenched French toast and fresh-baked breads. *Sheer perfection!*

CHETZEMOKA PARK

Follow Water Street east through downtown Port Townsend until it dead-ends just before the marina. Go north on Monroe Steet for seven short blocks and then east on Blaine for one block to the park.

I told a group of people I was off to explore romantic locations on the Olympic Peninsula. Within moments one of them slipped me a note that read: "There are parks and then there are parks, but there is only one Chetzemoka," and I agree. This ocean-flanked park makes picnicking a treasured outing for two people, particularly a couple who love surroundings that enhance the aesthetic appeal of cheese, fruit and wine. Here you can wander through scattered pinery along a cliff with an eagle's view of Admiralty Inlet and Whidbey Island. Thick grass, a footbridge over a babbling brook, a few well-spaced picnic tables, and swings make this traditional, picturesque park a standout. Whether your penchant is for a playful or a peaceful diversion, you will be pleased by Chetzemoka Park.

THE PAVILION, Port Townsend
628 Water Street
(206) 385-4881
Moderate to Expensive

On the north side of Water Street, in the heart of Port Townsend.

The Pavilion is a relatively new restaurant in Port Townsend, but it's likely to become one of the most romantic. The two-tiered, red-brick room in a tastefully renovated building is simply adorned with cloth-covered tables. The pace is easygoing but the food will arouse your emotions. Hearty French cuisine is what you'll find here. Menu items like thick, tender steak in a rich bechamel sauce, salmon cooked to perfection in a light bearnaise, and a moist veal dish are flavorful and nicely served. Polite service can be expected during the week, but on weekends you may feel somewhat hurried.

◆ *Romantic Option:* The waterfront view alternative to The Pavilion is just down the street in a narrow brick building that overlooks the ferries as they cruise to and from Whidbey Island on Admiralty Inlet. It's called **THE LIDO**, 925 Water Street, Port Townsend, (206) 385-7111 (Moderate) and is an attractive dining spot. Though the bar can be a bit smoky and noisy, the rest of the place is quiet and cozy. Hot fresh-baked bread, fresh pastas in light cream sauces, beautifully prepared salmon and a really good caesar salad are some of the items you'll find on the menu.

MANRESA CASTLE RESTAURANT & LOUNGE, Port Townsend
Seventh and Sheridan Streets
(206) 385-5750
Moderate to Expensive

From Highway 20 heading north, turn left onto Sheridan. Just before you enter the town of Port Townsend, the castle will be ahead of you on the right.

Manresa Castle was closed for awhile to undergo renovations that were supposed to have returned this esteemed mansion to its former brilliance and glory. Unfortunately, the only brilliance and glory to be found here is on the main floor where the restaurant and lounge are located. Both of these spots are thoroughly captivating. But the 36 rooms upstairs appear to have been left untouched except for some new bedspreads, televisions and Queen Anne-style dressers.

Even though I don't recommend an overnight stay, you will be enchanted by a lunch, dinner, or a drink here in the lounge. The stately cocktail lounge is a most irresistible setting for a romantic interlude, and next to it there's an unpretentious dining room where tall lace-covered windows, soft lighting and handsome wood furniture create an intimate, inviting atmosphere. The service is attentive and considerate, and the innovative Continental menu is wonderful.

DEER PARK

Deer Park is southeast of Port Angeles, in the Olympic National Park. From Highway 101 turn south at the sign for Deer Park. The park is at the end of this 17-mile drive.

My recommendation to make the drive to Deer Park comes with a warning. The countless switchbacks and sharp turns you'll encounter on this predominantly unpaved road will be hair-raising. With conditions like this, you need to be guaranteed that at the end there's a payoff. Rest assured there is, and suffer this road's indignities. The reward on a clear day is an enthralling view deep into the heartland of the Olympics. And because of the road conditions, you are likely to find yourselves quite alone. Most everyone else will drive the paved road to Hurricane Ridge (which has an absolutely astounding view of the Olympics) due south of Port Angeles just off Highway 101. The purple mountain majesty of Deer Park is all yours.

◆ **Romantic Note:** Ask at the ranger station (open in summer only) about the arduous hike up to Blue Mountain. Even your sore thighs will thank you for the view at the summit.

OLYMPIC HOT SPRINGS

Just southwest of Port Angeles on Highway 101, follow the signs to the Elwha campgrounds. Stay on this road past the ranger station and for another four miles around Lake Mills. There the road will dead-end. Park your car along the side of the road, where you are likely to see a handful of other parked vehicles. The old road ahead, now in disuse, continues for 2.4 miles uphill to the hot springs.

I don't understand why people in the Northwest seem to be infatuated with soaking in outdoor hot tubs fashioned by nature. Even when these bubbling springs of earth-heated water are located in the midst of piercingly beautiful scenery, the piercing smell of sulphur is enough to make you sick. And then there's the problem of running into people you'd never want to share your bathtub with. I'll take a chlorinated Jacuzzi hot tub any day.

Well, in spite of all this, my aquatic husband and my non-aquatic self ventured up to Olympic Hot Springs on his insistence that I didn't know what I was missing and that I would be doing a disservice to my readers if I didn't tell them about the wonders of simmering in a mud-bottomed, smelly pool of lava-heated water.

The uphill walk passed through forest, and that was wonderful. And because we started late in the day, we saw a number of drip-drying people heading back who gave us words of encouragement: "Not much farther," "It's great, keep going." As we crossed a log bridge over the effervescent waters of the Elwha River, the aroma of the nearby springs hit me like a lead balloon. The stone-and-log pools were terraced along a hillside. When my husband saw this he joyfully ran ahead, stripped down to his swimsuit, and enthusiastically plunged in.

When I finally took the plunge I was surprised at how clean the water looked. The water that surges up from the earth's center constantly replaces the "used" water which spills over the rim. The bottom wasn't all that muddy, though yes, the odor was omnipresent and offensive. But to my amazement, my skin did feel silky smooth and we didn't see another person the entire time we were there.

So, do I think it's romantic? Well, my husband does — I guess that's half the battle.

LAKE CRESCENT
LAKE CRESCENT LODGE

**Olympic National Forest
Highway 101
(206) 928-3211**
Moderate to Expensive

On the northern edge of the Olympic National Park, accessible just off Highway 101. When you approach Lake Crescent, look for signs indicating the way to the lodge. (The lodge is closed October 29th through April 29th.)

A sunny day here may wreak havoc with your senses and emotions. Lake Crescent Lodge rests on the bank of the enormous lake and from your white-shingled cabin — heated by a woodstove or a stone fireplace — you can view this glassy stretch of water as it curves around forested mountains that ascend magnificently in the distance. Inhale deeply the fragrant air that permeates this epic landscape. The bond you and your loved one forge amid all this beauty will be strong and everlasting.

If you're just passing through, stop at the Lodge's attractive restaurant and savor a traditional mountain breakfast with robust fresh coffee (a rare find outside of a major city or town), a wholesome lunch or a selection of dinner items ranging from king salmon to Hood Canal oysters in a smooth remoulade.

◆ *Romantic Note:* The most romantic accommodations at the lodge are the Roosevelt Fireplace Cottages.

◆ *Second Romantic Note:* The drive around the perimeter of the lake is a monumental treat. (Be sure to check seasonal accessibility.) Take the time to see the whole thing and refresh yourself with a swim in summer or an energetic hike at other times of the year.

CAPE FLATTERY

Highway 101 intersects Highway 112 a few miles west of Port Angeles. Take Highway 112 west along the coast to the town of Sekiu. Twenty miles beyond Sekiu to the west is Neah Bay, and Cape Flattery is 8.5 miles northwest of there.

Sekiu is a small unassuming fishing village with a handful of motels lining the dock. The town is only 28.5 miles from the northwestern tip of the continental United States, which makes it the gateway to some of the most scintillating scenery anywhere. Drive ahead to Neah Bay just so you can gaze along the Strait of Juan de Fuca, flanked on one side by shoreline and rugged inlets, and on the other by Vancouver Island's striking mountainous profile. But don't stop here, the best is yet to come.

Drive farther northwest to Cape Flattery. Here you can camp or just stop long enough to embrace and behold nightfall. A 30-minute hike down a wooded trail brings you to an astounding corner of the world. Your city temperaments will mellow as you watch the cinematic sunset over the rock-strewn beach and the fall of dusk on Tatoosh Island.

SHI SHI BEACH

Drive seven miles southwest of Neah Bay until you come to something that resembles a parking area with signs for the beach. Look over the embankment adjacent to this parking lot and you will see an expansive, empty beach on Makah Bay. Hike from the parking lot through three miles of forest and beach trail to Shi Shi.

In its magnitude and overwhelming presence, this eight-mile stretch of untainted beach rivals any along the entire west coast of the United States. There really are no adjectives equal to the task of describing hundreds of seastacks, cliffs, forest, sand and waves. This place needs to be seen to be believed. And because it takes a bit of stamina to get there, you might find yourselves alone at the edge of the world.

THIRD BEACH

Follow the signs on Highway 101 to LaPush, on the northwestern coast of the Olympic Penninsula. There is only one road that goes south of LaPush along the coast. Two miles down this road there is a small, barely noticeable sign indicating Third Beach and an unmarked parking area at the trailhead. A ³/₄-mile walk on a forest path brings you to the beach.

A dear friend introduced me to Third Beach several summers ago. He said that when his city life gets too crazy, he reclaims his sanity in the wilderness, and Third Beach is one of his favorite places to go and do that. When I arrived there I understood why.

You can run barefoot for two miles along this surf-pounded beach of firm sand, and there are hidden caves and rock formations to explore along the way. At low tide you can climb onto what at high tide were islands and marvel at tidepools full of trapped sealife. As is true with any angel-sent outing, day's end will come too soon; be sure to take a seashell or some weather-aged pebbles back home with you as a keepsake of your beautiful time together.

HOH RAIN FOREST, Olympic National Forest

On Highway 101 south of Forks, on the northwest side of the Olympic National Forest, look for signs directing you to the Hoh Visitor Center, (206) 374-6925, which is 19 miles east of the highway. Inquire there about the hikes available at your skill level.

The Hoh Rain Forest displays what Mother Nature can do when she has an abundance of moisture (150 inches of rain annually) to thrive on. Every inch of ground, including decaying trees, is covered with moss, lichens, mushrooms, ferns and sorrel. As you pass under this forest canopy, you will also see some of the largest spruce, fir and cedar trees that exist in the world. There are moss-laden evergreens here 300 feet tall and 23 feet around. On a rare sunny day, streams of light penetrate the thick foliage in a golden misty haze. Don't even try to restrain the joy and excitement you'll feel with every step. And since you can't restrain the moisture that oozes from the ground, be certain to wear waterproof shoes.

KALALOCH LODGE, Forks
Highway 101
(206) 962-2271
Inexpensive to Moderate

The village of Kalaloch lies northwest of Quinault and south of the Hoh River Valley. The lodge is on the west side of the road directly off Highway 101.

The Pacific Ocean is Kalaloch's front-yard entertainment and the primary reason to be here. During low tide, the walk along the shore is a long, sandy hike accompanied by seagulls drifting overhead. At high tide, the ocean surf resounds in the air. In order to spend enough time to enjoy all tidal phases, you may wish to stay overnight in the eclectic assortment of accommodations here. The main lodge has 9 adequate, airy rooms and a mediocre oceanside restaurant. Further down, on a bluff overlooking the ocean, there are 16 newer, cedar-wood cabins and 6 older, rustic log cabins. Several of these have fireplaces, all are very comfortable and roomy, and most have views of the sovereign sunsets and an ethereal seascape. Close by, there's a fairly new motel-style building with another 10 units, most of which have wonderful views, fireplaces, sliding glass doors, and lots of room. Regardless of where you choose to stay, in the evening after dinner, light a fire, turn the lights down low and launch into a night of ghost stories, giggling and cuddling.

LAKE QUINAULT LODGE, Quinault
South Shore Road
(206) 288-2571
Inexpensive to Moderate

South of the Village of Kalaloch on Highway 101, turn east on South Shore Road. Proceed two miles to the lodge.

This isn't the fanciest lodge you will ever visit, unless you think video games in the bar and faux fireplaces in the guestrooms are fancy, and you may want to call first to be sure a convention group isn't booked at the same time you are. You'll also want to reserve a place in the older section of the lodge where the rooms are quaint but small, and think twice about the newer units which are comfortable but have an ultra-tacky decor. Still, there are details that make Lake Quinault Lodge fairly enticing. What more could someone with tender intentions require than a grand, cedar-shingle rustic lodge with a massive stone fireplace in the lobby? Or a view of a mountain lake cradled by the evolutionary masterpiece, the Olympic Rain Forest? Not enough? Add to that numerous eerily intriguing hikes to explore after a relaxed breakfast or lunch. (Be sure to order the standard items from the menu; this restaurant doesn't do well if it has to mix more than three ingredients at a time.) And on a clear day, include a lake cruise just before sunset. Still something missing? Just nuzzle together to quickly forget which way lies civilization and realize that sometimes a location like this and your certain someone are all you really need.

> *"Love is the most precious thing in the world.*
> *Whatever figures in second place*
> *doesn't even come close."*
>
> **Ann Landers**

WASHINGTON STATE ISLANDS

SAN JUAN ISLANDS

*Several of the islands are accessible by ferryboat from Anacortes. For information on departure times, call the **Washington State Ferries** at (206) 464-6400; or toll free (800) 542-7052.*

There are 172 islands in the San Juan archipelago, each with a stunning terrain, a distinctive character, and some with bustling villages. As you circumnavigate the most popular island grouping by ferryboat—Orcas Island, San Juan Island, and Lopez Island—you may be reminded of the island-dotted Caribbean, a notable difference being that the San Juans are much more spectacular in their topography. Of course, you won't see any palm trees here, and since you're about as far north as you can go in the continental United States, the blush on your cheeks will be from the cold and not the equatorial heat. But so much the better: cool cheeks give you a snuggling advantage.

Deciding on the one ideal destination won't be an easy task. You can opt for the comfort of the more populated islands, or if you own or have chartered a boat, you can homestead on one of the lesser-known islands, setting up camp for a more back-to-basics holiday. Wherever you put down roots, you'll be happy.

◆ ***Romantic Note:*** To save a lot of time and frustration, check with the **Outdoor Recreation Information Center**, (206) 442-0170 and **Washington State Parks**, (800) 562-0990. They can lead you in the right direction for outdoor activities and campgrounds. Always check seasonal hours and rates whenever you choose a restaurant or island accommodation.

◆ ***Romantic Suggestion:*** Before you get on the ferryboat you should consider stopping in for a meal at the elegantly renovated **MAJESTIC HOTEL**, 419 Commercial Avenue, (206) 293-3355 (Moderate to Expensive) in downtown Anacortes. The hotel has a European-style pub that is simply enchanting and offers good, light fare. But it's the atmosphere you'll savor most of all. The main restaurant was not yet open at the time this book went to press. It seemed nice enough, but I was disappointed to see the boxes of packaged pasta from Costco laid out on the counter with other prepackaged items. You will not be disappointed, however, if you decide to spend a night at the hotel. The rooms are charming, meticulously decorated in a bright, floral country motif, a tad small and expensive, but nonetheless lovely.

LONESOME COVE RESORT, San Juan Island

5810-A Lonesome Cove Road, Friday Harbor
(206) 378-4477
Moderate to Expensive

From the ferry dock at Friday Harbor, follow the signs to Roche Harbor. Just before you enter Roche Harbor, turn right on Rouleau Road. Two miles east of Roche Harbor turn right at Limestone Point Road and then left on Lonesome Cove Road.

Rustic living is offered here with secluded island comfort. The cabins reside on a sandy beach, built 20 feet beyond the high-tide mark. Lonesome Cove is backed by several acres of dense forest that open onto a clearing of manicured lawns extending down to the water. This is an irresistible place for an arm-in-arm walk, and there are trees, beach and rocks to explore.

The cabins are assembled like village hideaways and they are all genuinely homespun. Their prime assets are fireplaces and big glass windows that overlook Speiden Channel, Speiden Island, and off in the distance, Vancouver Island. By the way, the name of this resort is misleading; with the right someone, lonesomeness here is unthinkable.

OLYMPIC LIGHTS BED & BREAKFAST,
San Juan Island

4531-A Cattlepoint Road, Friday Harbor
(206) 378-3186
Inexpensive to Moderate

From the ferry landing at Friday Harbor, follow Spring Street to Argyle Road and turn left at the dead-end. Then turn right onto Cattle Point Road. The road will veer left, but stay on it. Just before you come to American Camp you'll see a little sign for Olympic Lights. Turn right to the house.

Generally, I hesitate to recommend a bed & breakfast where the rooms share baths, for all the obvious unromantic reasons. But Olympic Lights is worth making an exception to my rule, and once you experience it you'll know why. In what seems to be the middle of nowhere, you'll find this house sitting on a pristine meadow overlooking the nearby water and mountains. The feeling of serenity here is practically guaranteed.

The interior of this sparkling clean Victorian home is whimsically appointed: soft-sculptured rabbits entwined in gold stars fill the rooms, along with some very unusual artwork. There is a lovely room on the ground level right off the kitchen with its own bath, but the rooms that share two baths upstairs are really wonderful. The Ra Room (named after the Egyptian sun god) is eminently comfortable, and the morning sun pours through the windows onto your well-rested faces. You won't have to leave the downy white bed to see dawn break over the waving fields and the bay. But do get up in time to indulge in the lavish farm-fresh breakfast.

◆ **Romantic Note:** When you arrive at Olympic Lights you will be asked to remove your shoes before going upstairs to your room—and the reason is crystal clear. The upper level is completely covered with snow-white carpeting.

◆ **Romantic Suggestion:** While you're on San Juan Island, be sure to visit **WHALE PARK** on the eastern shore. Two pods of whales make regular trips through this area. It is from this spot that you're most likely to see these enormous creatures cavorting in play. But even if you don't have a sighting here, you'll probably witness a sensational sunset with the bay in the foreground and the white-peaked Olympic Mountains in the distance. This is a wondrous, often private section of the island.

WESTWINDS BED & BREAKFAST,
San Juan Island

4909-H Hannah Highlands Road, Friday Harbor
(206) 378-5283
Moderate

Call for reservations and directions.

After I describe this perfect island retreat to you, please don't be angry about there being only one suite available; this place is still not all that well-known and you may have a chance at a reservation. Westwinds is a wood-and-glass home that rests high atop a hill in the middle of the island. From up here you'll feel as if you can see to eternity, and the view is a significant part of the house's interior design. Your room is large and tastefully designed with French doors that open to a private deck where you can loll away the morning over breakfast, which is more than just a cornucopia of delights; it is also artistically presented and lovingly served. This is a truly commendable, one-of-a-kind island getaway.

◆ *Romantic Alternative:* A new contemporary bed & breakfast called **TRUMPETER INN**, 420 Trumpeter Way, (206) 378-3884, (Inexpensive to Moderate) rests in a pastoral valley just outside the town of Friday Harbor. The name honors the real-life trumpeter swans which glide across the nearby ponds. This is a genuinely private getaway with views in the distance of False Bay and the Olympic Mountains beyond the Strait. Every room is brightly decorated and exceptionally comfortable, with private baths, down comforters, and the sounds of the countryside's own natural music. In the morning a lavish breakfast is served on the deck or in the dining room.

DUCK SOUP INN, San Juan Island
3090 Roche Harbor Road, Friday Harbor
(206) 378-4878
Moderate

Take the ferryboat from Anacortes to Friday Harbor on San Juan Island. The ferry traffic exits onto Spring Street. Turn right onto Second, and follow the signs to Roche Harbor Road. Heading north on Roche Harbor Road, continue for five miles to the restaurant.

On San Juan Island there are two well-established dining places that pose a dilemma for hungry lovebirds. Both Duck Soup Inn and Winston's (see entry this section) boast gourmet eating opportunities; both have wonderful but very different atmospheres. If your tastebuds and hearts long for a rustic Northwest motif and savory fresh entrees that change daily, Duck Soup Inn is your answer. The restaurant is a wood-frame country home totally removed from the tourist trail. The country decor and relaxed service make for an easy, pleasant evening.

ROCHE HARBOR RESORT RESTAURANT,
San Juan Island
P.O. Box 4001, Roche Harbor
(206) 378-2155
Moderate to Expensive

From Anacortes, take the ferry to Friday Harbor. At the ferry dock follow the traffic up Spring Street and turn right at Second Street. At Tucker Avenue turn right again and stay to your left at the fork; this will put you on Roche Harbor Road. You will come to a "T" eight miles down this road, where you turn right and drive to the village of Roche Harbor. Turn left at the arches to the resort.

This historic harbor and marina is a yachting playground. Every inch of the area that isn't lined with boats is covered with gazebos, rose gardens, sculpted hedges and ivy-laden buildings. Winding brick pathways weave through this New Englandesque resort. Roche Harbor Restaurant is San Juan Island's premier port of call. You will be inclined to dally for a while on the deck over morning coffee or afternoon tea. When the restaurant is open, the handsome interior, gentle harbor view and well-prepared seafood will encourage you to make an entire day of it. This is indeed a reposeful spot from which to watch the comings and goings in the scenic, barrier-island-protected marina.

◆ *Romantic Warning:* The main hotel is old and musty, and the newer, expensive rental condos down the road are okay but nothing to write home about. Consider staying instead at Lonesome Cove or Westwinds and enjoying a meal or two here at Roche Harbor.

SPRINGTREE EATING ESTABLISHMENT AND FARM, San Juan Island ◆◆◆

310 Spring Street
(206) 378-4848
Inexpensive to Moderate

In Friday Harbor, at the top of Spring Street, under a very large elm tree.

The Springtree restaurant is simply adorable and unique. The white picket-fence entrance is draped by a sprawling elm tree that covers the entire red-brick courtyard. It took some powerful shears to cut back this mighty arbor. Inside everything is equally as charming and casual, with floor-to-ceiling French windows that keep the interior bright in the daytime and cozy at night. The food is country-fresh; much of the produce and herbs are picked from the privately owned farm referred to in the restaurant's name. Every dish is flawlessly prepared, with great care given to perfecting the art of Northwest cuisine.

WINSTON'S, San Juan Island
95 Nichols, Friday Harbor
(206) 378-4073
Moderate

As you exit the ferry dock at Friday Harbor, follow Spring Street and turn right onto Nichols. The restaurant is two blocks west of the ferry dock.

Winston's is a subdued two-story Victorian renovation in the heart of Friday Harbor. It has a "Gatsbyish" feel to it that is inviting and attractive. The interior is done in soft pastels with flickering candles illuminating the dimly lit room. The menu runs the gamut from standard continental fare to exotic ethnic specialties. This restaurant exemplifies relaxed island sophistication, and if you choose to dine at Winston's, your palatal needs will be beautifully tended to.

AMERICAN CAMP, San Juan Island

From Friday Harbor, follow the ferry traffic on Spring Street to Argyle Road and turn left. This road jogs around to become Cattle Point Road, where you turn left again and proceed directly to American Camp.

The heavily forested terrain in the northern section of San Juan Island gives way to windswept leas carpeted with poppies, wildflowers and waving waist-high grass at the island's southern extremity, called American Camp. Once you arrive your options are to walk down to the enormous sandy beach and investigate the shoreline and cold Sound waters, or to meander through the spacious meadows that are a mix of sandhills and seagrass. The many opportunities for ducking out of sight make this a perfect camp for lovers. From your personal nook on a cliff, or as you wander along mesmerized by the glorious view of the Olympics, you can watch the sun's procession from morning to dusk as it bathes the hills in a rainbow of colors.

◆ **Romantic Alternative:** If you have the energy and a good pair of shoes, don't miss climbing the beautiful uphill trail from

ENGLISH CAMP to YOUNG HILL. The view will astound you, as will the peace and solitude. You may find yourselves sharing this spectacle with the soaring eagles that make their home in this paradise. You may also come to understand why so many people say that San Juan Island is the Garden of Eden. Leave yourselves at least an hour for this round-trip jaunt.

DEER HARBOR INN, Orcas Island

P.O. Box 142, Deer Harbor

(206) 376-4110

Inexpensive

As you drive off the ferry, turn left. Go three miles and turn left on the first paved road past the ferry landing. After one more mile you will drive by West Sound. Continue four miles, and you'll see the sign for Deer Harbor Inn on the left.

High on a grassy knoll overlooking Deer Harbor and the surrounding forested hillside, there's a contemporary, beautifully constructed log cabin bed & breakfast. Each airy room has its own bath and cozy furnishings. The rooms aren't eleborate, but they are inviting and very comfortable, with wood-framed beds that are somehow soft and perfectly firm at the same time. There are outdoor decks, and a morning picnic basket is delivered to your room each day. The sitting areas have fresh coffee brewing all day and there is plenty of peace and quiet to be found here.

A short stroll from the inn is DEER HARBOR RESTAURANT. The spacious, country dining room has rustic charm and a down-home atmosphere. The food is remarkably fresh and the portions are hearty and generous. This is not where you come for nouvelle cuisine. The service is considerate and friendly and everything seems to be paced just right. For an island getaway, this place richly deserves its rating.

♦ *Romantic Suggestion:* At Deer Harbor Resort, down the road a few miles from Deer Harbor Inn, there's a boat rental service called

DEER HARBOR CHARTERS, (206) 376-5989. They have small boats that you can take to a nearby private island, water taxis that travel between here and Friday Harbor on San Juan Island, yacht charters with or without a captain, dazzling sunset sails with refreshments, entertaining dinner cruises, scuba diving lessons and more.

NORTH SHORE COTTAGES, Orcas Island
P.O. Box 1273, Eastsound
(206) 376-5131
Moderate

Call for reservations and directions to the cottages.

This place provided one of the most romantic evenings I've ever experienced in the Northwest — and given that I do this kind of thing on a regular basis, that's really saying something. Of course I don't want to give all the credit to the rustically handsome cabin we stayed in, called the Artist's Studio, or the private outdoor deck with a hot tub overlooking the Canadian Gulf Islands and the glistening waters of the Strait of Georgia. I mean, even the stone fireplace, comfortable, quilt-covered bed, and the large bay window that provided a majestic view can't account for all the enchantment in the air and the smile on our faces. After all, some of the credit goes to us for what we made of our surroundings. But far be it from me to suggest that all of those details didn't contribute to the evening we shared at North Shore Cottages.

◆ *Romantic Note:* This is not a bed & breakfast, though the cabin does have a small, fully equipped kitchen. There is also another cabin on the property that is larger and set further back from the edge of the cliff. It is nice, too, but nowhere near as romantic as the Artist's Studio in which we stayed.

ORCAS HOTEL, Orcas Island
P.O. Box 155
(206) 376-4300
Inexpensive to Expensive

Just above the Orcas Island ferry dock.

"Hotel" is really a misnomer here, since that term often conjures up an image of a sterile building with identical rooms and basic detailing, none of which applies to this striking, three-story Victorian inn. The view from the wraparound windows in the dining room and lounge — and from many of the rooms upstairs — is striking. From this vantage point you can watch the comings and goings around Harney Channel, Wasp Passage and Shaw Island.

Actually, this 1904 landmark has only two rooms to offer in the way of kissing-preferred accommodations. Most of the other rooms are on the small side, and only those on the third floor have their own bathrooms, which are all smallish too (after all, this is an old building). But the two new suites, called "Romantic Rooms," are just that — completely romantic. French doors open onto a private deck, the bathrooms have Jacuzzis built for two, and the bedrooms are lovely and comfortable. The pricetag is a bit steep for these spots — some of the most expensive on the island — but after all, this is a special occasion we're talking about, isn't it? To help ease the strain on your pocketbook, a full breakfast served in the hotel's restaurant is included in the rate. Any meal in this window-framed country-perfect dining room will be a pleasure, and the food, though basic, is quite good.

◆ *Romantic Note:* Since this hotel is located at the foot of the ferry dock, there is exceptionally heavy traffic of tourists and cars during the summer season. And the downstairs public rooms can get crowded when there is a delay in boarding the ferry.

SAND DOLLAR INN, Orcas Island
P.O. Box 152, Olga
(206) 376-5696
Inexpensive to Moderate

Call for reservations and directions.

As you travel the horseshoe-shaped main road of Orcas Island you pass miles of forest, inlets, coves, lakes, and composed villages and country neighborhoods. Sand Dollar Inn is located in the midst of all that scenery. From the outside, this wood-framed, ordinary country home appears to be nice enough, though not necessarily a great island hideaway. Once inside, however, tucked safely in your room, romance and loving solitude are yours for the asking. There are three rooms upstairs with soft down comforters, sweeping views, light-wood furnishings, white linens and private baths. Your morning meal is served on the glass-enclosed deck that looks out to the hills and water. During our visit we watched eagles dart in and out of the water trying to get a bit of breakfast themselves. This is a comfortable, soothing island spot where you will find respite from the stress and strain of city life.

TURTLEBACK FARM INN, Orcas Island
Route 1, Box 650, Eastsound
(206) 376-4914
Inexpensive to Moderate

From the ferry dock follow Horseshoe Highway and turn left on McNallie Road. At Crow Valley Road turn right and watch for the sign indicating the inn.

When the sun begins to warm the air and the colors of the countryside come alive with the glow of daybreak, Turtleback Inn is a delightful place to be. Every corner of this old farmhouse has been painstakingly renovated by people who clearly were sensitive to the landscape which surrounds it. The rooms and private baths range from charming to more charming (though the less expensive rooms are rather small). The pastoral setting — 80 acres of hills, pasture, ponds, and meadow — will warm your hearts, as will the plentiful breakfast served at your own table in the window-framed dining room. The likelihood is that you will be wholeheartedly pleased with your stay here.

BILBO'S FESTIVO, Orcas Island
North Beach Road, Eastsound
(206) 376-4728
Inexpensive

In the town of Eastsound, at A Street and North Beach Road.

How is it possible that such a very tiny village as Eastsound can have so many excellent restaurants? Each one at which we've dined serves incredible dinners that are fresh and distinctive, with truly outstanding flavors and presentations. One of our favorites, Bilbo's, is a charming Mexican restaurant with wooden, hand-tiled benches, stone fireplace and soft lighting. Outside there is a courtyard garden with a blazing firepit in the center surrounded by outdoor seating. The food is authentic and light, mildly spicy, with generous portions. This is a local favorite, so reservations are a good idea, and so is a Mexican beer while you wait for your table.

CHRISTINA'S, Orcas Island
Horseshoe Highway, Eastsound
(206) 376-4904
Moderate to Expensive

At the intersection of North Beach Road and Horseshoe Highway.

Christina's is even more impressive than its highly acclaimed reputation led us to believe. We dined over fresh local clams, superb moist salmon, and a creamy pasta dish that was sheer heaven. The setting was island elegance, set right on the waterfront. From the glass-enclosed porch there are stunning views of the mountains surrounding the Eastsound inlet. On a sunny summer day the rooftop terrace is an alluring setting for lunch or dinner.

ROSARIO ISLAND RESORT RESTAURANT, Orcas Island

One Rosario Way, Eastsound
(206) 376-2222
Moderate to Expensive

From the ferryboat landing go north on Horseshoe Highway to Eastsound, loop around the water and head south. Rosario Resort is about five miles down the road.

I would not be the first or the last person to rave about Rosario Resort's location and views. And I would not be the only person to warn you about the accommodations, which are very expensive and in desperate need of renovation. I'm also probably not the first to comment on the restaurant, but I can't resist: having a corner table, near the floor-to-ceiling windows that expose a sparkling view of the area, is enough to fill anyone's heart for the day or night. Yes, the food is American-standard and just slightly better than ordinary, but the service is adequate and they try hard. Then there's that view! All in all, Rosario is a good enough place for a morning or afternoon time-out from your day's activities; dinner is too expensive to be worth it, and the rooms don't even remotely justify the expense.

THE BUNGALOW RESTAURANT, Orcas Island

A Street, Eastsound
(206) 376-4338
Moderate to Expensive

In the heart of the town of Eastsound, on the main street.

The Bungalow is a newly renovated waterfront restaurant with a ringside, unobstructed view of Eastsound Inlet, which in itself is a major esthetic plus. The menu is a mouth-watering listing of such things as fresh halibut poached in champagne and mint butter, local cod baked in tomato basil butter, and blackened black-tip shark served with a red-pepper sage sauce. The desserts are worth every frustrating calorie. Perhaps a bit too formal for an island setting, but maybe in time the management will loosen up and stop trying so hard.

◆ *Romantic Possibility:* LA FAMIGLIA, A Street, (206) 376-2335, (Inexpensive to Moderate) is a bit more family-oriented (as the name suggests) than Bilbo's or Christina's, but when you have to have pasta, the craving needs to be satisfied and this is the best place to do it for miles around. You'll find a simple interior here, sedate lighting, fresh pasta and rich flavorful sauces. Not the most romantic spot in town, but the fettuccini will satisfy your pasta cravings. Then you can take care of the rest of your needs.

ISLAND KAYAK GUIDES, Orcas Island
Doe Bay Village, Olga
(206) 376-2291
Moderate

Call for directions and detailed information about your trip.

The brochure said "no experience necessary." It's not that I'm a wimp, it's just that I'm not much of a swimmer, and the idea of paddling the cold waters around the islands seemed not only dangerous but exhausting, and as far removed from romantic as one can get. The staff assured me that instructions in paddling and the use of the equipment would be thorough and that the trip would be geared to my skill level. Great, I said, that would mean I'd be stuck paddling around the dock for an hour. They insisted nothing of the sort had ever happened before, and I was encouraged to be open-minded and give it a try. Okay, but just this once.

Wouldn't you know it? Now I can't wait to do it again! There is something quite remarkable about propelling yourselves in a two-person kayak through the open waters around the forested islands of the San Juans. It's exciting to be an actual part of nature's aquatic playground, where eagles and seabirds swoop down across the water's surface, otters and seals dart in and out of the current and, on occasion, a great orca effortlessly glides by. There are no words to describe the sensation of watching the world from this vantage point, and the strength of your arms (or lack of it) has little bearing on the quality of the experience. All kinds of special trips are possible, some that include time for picnicking, sunbathing and island exploration. Whichever one you choose, you won't regret giving it your best shot.

MOUNT CONSTITUTION, Orcas Island

From the ferryboat landing, go north on Horseshoe Highway to the town of Eastsound. Loop around the Sound and head south, following signs to the mountain, which is in the center of Moran State Park.

The road into Moran State Park will lead you to the tallest elevation on the Washington islands, Mount Constitution. Its easily attained summit is a stone-work lookout tower well above the treetops. From Mount Constitution's peak you have a stupendous 360-degree view of this part of the Northwest. To the east are the majestic Cascades; to the north, the Gulf Islands demand your attention; to the west, looming on the horizon, are the Olympics; to the south are the San Juan Islands; and above is the endless blue sky. There is wonderful camping to be found up here. Unquestionably, Mt. Constitution is one of the more spectacular spots on the islands.

◆ *Romantic Note:* Mount Constitution is a well-visited frontier. For a less-touristed experience, hike the mountaintop trails and claim a landmark of your own.

◆ *Romantic Suggestion:* CAFÉ OLGA, Star Route Box 155, (206) 376-4408 (Inexpensive) is a few miles south of Mount Constitution, located in the Orcas Island Artworks store. The atmosphere is laid back, with strong overtones of the late '60s, but the food is anything but laid back. Exceptional dishes like Sicilian artichoke pie, a creamy rich manicotti with walnuts, and Moroccan salad brimming with couscous, dates, almonds and spices are just a sampling from this one-of-a-kind menu. Leisurely dining is what you'll find in this rustic setting, and you'll have ample time to share your thoughts and get to know each other a little better.

EDENWILD INN, Lopez Island

In Lopez Village
(206) 468-3238
Moderate to Expensive

From the ferry landing follow the signs to Lopez Village. The inn is located on the main road in town (there is only one), Lopez Road South.

This inn is an ambitious undertaking for Lopez Island. Prior to the building of this sparkling new, very contemporary, totally elegant, upscale bed & breakfast, a visitor to Lopez would have found only rustic, down-home accommodations. Now with the opening of Edenwild all that has changed and, depending on your point of view, it is a beautiful, thoroughly romantic addition to the area. There are 7 rooms here all brightly decorated, some with fireplaces, some with views, all with private baths and all utterly distinctive places to stay. Breakfast is a generous display of fresh baked-egg dishes, pastries and breads. To some people, the Edenwild may seem a bit slick for this semi-remote island, but for us it was the perfect compromise between getting away from it all and having the amenities we both enjoy.

LANGLEY, Whidbey Island

Thirty miles north of Seattle, take the Mukilteo ferry to the town of Clinton on Whidbey Island. The town of Langley is five miles north on Highway 525.

People with an unromantic disposition may describe Langley as a one-horse town. And they'd be right. It just depends on what kind of horse they had in mind. Langley is a town that still exhibits a Northwest look and style without compromising its virtues just to attract tourists. There is nothing in the vicinity for miles around to spoil the scenery. Of course, over the years the main street has become a bit yuppified, but that still doesn't get in the way of the original ambience of the area.

Langley sits on the water's edge, and from its meadows and bluffs there are amazing views of Mount Baker, the Cascades and the Saratoga Passage. The appeal of this town lies in the unaffected style of its buildings and shops, which are quaint and charming. As you travel through Whidbey Island, don't let yourselves miss a visit to this extraordinary place.

◆ *Romantic Options:* The accommodations in Langley, hands down, are some of the best places for affection and romance I have seen anywhere. There are almost too many to mention. My absolute favorites, which makes for a very long list, are as follows, in alphabetical order:

COUNTRY COTTAGE OF LANGLEY, Whidbey Island

215 Sixth Street, Langley (206) 221-8709
Inexpensive

From the ferry dock follow Highway 525 into Langley, turn right on Maxwelton Road, bear left onto Langley Road which becomes Cascade. Turn left on 6th Street to the cottage.

This is a lovely, country-elegant home just a few blocks from town. The rooms are more like suites where the nights can be filled with fantasy and country relaxation. There are two detached guestrooms with private entrances and a porch overlooking the water and mountains. A large deck wraps around a well-tended garden from which you'll also see the water and mountains. The breakfast service is great.

EAGLE'S NEST BED & BREAKFAST, Whidbey Island
3236 East Saratoga Road, Langley (206) 321-5331
Moderate

From the ferry dock follow Highway 525 into Langley, turn right on Maxwelton Road, bear left onto Langley Road which becomes Cascade. Turn left on 2nd Street which becomes Saratoga Road.

This newly constructed home sits high on a hill on the outskirts of Langley. The views from the deck and the hot tub are, without exaggeration, spectacular. The house is huge and the four rooms spacious and brightly decorated. Some have balconies, private entries and views, and all are a great place to call home for a few days of time alone. When you wake in the morning, you'll find a tray of juice and coffee waiting outside your door, followed by a home-cooked breakfast (and the cookie jar is never empty).

THE INN AT LANGLEY, Whidbey Island
400 First Street, Langley
(206) 221-3033
Moderate to Expensive

From the ferry dock follow Highway 525 into Langley, turn right on Maxwelton Road, bear left onto Langley Road which becomes Cascade which becomes First Street.

The Inn at Langley is the newest addition to this town's burgeoning list of acclaimed accommodations. And this one is the sleekest and most tempting of them all. The building is set high on a bluff overlooking Saratoga Passage. Each of the 24 rooms has a glorious view of the mountains and water. There are private decks, wood-burning fireplaces, thick comforters, terrycloth robes, and a large tiled bathroom that I would give anything to move into my home. The deep two-person spa tub is fronted by a shower area the size of a small room. Both are precisely placed to face the view and the fire. There is even access to the beach below. According to the inn's brochure, "the heart of the inn is the formal country kitchen," and they couldn't be more accurate. A generous continental breakfast is served in the morning, and a Northwest epicurean production is served at night to guests and visitors alike (by reservation).

LONE LAKE COTTAGE & BREAKFAST,
Whidbey Island
5206 South Bayview Road, Langley (206) 321-5325
Moderate

From the ferry dock follow Highway 525 for 5½ miles and turn right onto Bayview Road. Drive for one mile to the cottage, which will appear on your left.

Everything about Lone Lake Cottage is enchanting and unique. This eclectic assortment of accommodations, five miles outside of town, is the most inventive place to stay in Langley. The innkeepers have built a striking, professionally designed aviary, complete with incubators and waterfall, the likes of which you'd expect to see only in a zoo. There are fascinating, colorful birds from all over the world in this immaculately maintained walk-in menagerie, and down by the lake there are black swans and exotic ducks to watch.

Two of the three units here are uniquely charming cottages with fully equipped kitchens well-stocked with breakfast treats, fireplaces, private decks overlooking the lake, VCRs, stereos, cozy dining nooks, and warm sitting areas. One of the units even has a black spa tub with a skylight over it. For a real change of pace, stay on the one-of-a-kind glass-enclosed houseboat with a darling galley and walk-up queen-size bed. Each place is a total escape, and the setting is totally peaceful. Lone Lake doesn't mean alone; it means that you two have only your loving selves for company.

THE LOVELY COTTAGE, Whidbey Island

4130 East Lovely Road, Clinton
(206) 321-6592
Moderate

From the ferry dock follow Highway 525 to Cultus Bay Road and turn south, staying on Cultus Bay Road until you reach Lovely Road. Then turn left to the cottage.

I dislike cute names, but in this case I'll make an exception, because The Lovely Cottage is not only lovely, it is wonderful. Nestled into a two-acre oceanfront homestead, the cottage is a quaint, endearing place to spend time in total privacy. The view from your private porch, sweeping lawn and gardens is nothing less than breathtaking. The snowpeaked Olympics towering over the horizon and the sky's changing countenance as the sun sets are right there for your personal entertainment. There is even a huge hot tub for your own personal use in the backyard. Inside, the cottage is an eclectic blend of rustic, cozy furnishings and a full kitchen. The massive stairway down to the beach is a work of engineering ingenuity.

◆ *Romantic Alternative:* SERENITY PINES CLIFF COTTAGE, (206) 321-5005 (Moderate) is a small, attractive, self-contained cottage set on a forested bluff, overlooking a soothing view of the Saratoga Passage and the Cascade Mountains. The contemporary interior is pretty and has all the conveniences of home including a full kitchen, wood-stove and petite dining area. Sliding glass doors open onto a private deck that has a hot tub providing a warm vantage point from which you can better enjoy the view. The cottage is one of the many properties mananged by **NORTHWEST VACATION HOMES.** Most of their other properties are better suited for families and not couples looking for a romantic hideaway.

THE WHIDBEY INN BED & BREAKFAST, Whidbey Island

106 First Street, Langley (206) 221-7115
Moderate to Expensive

From the ferry dock follow Highway 525 into Langley. Turn right on Maxwelton Road, then bear left on Langley Road which becomes Cascade which becomes First Street.

Reputedly one of Whidbey Island's finest, this inn assuredly ranks among the most interesting and elegant. In the heart of Langley, it resides on a bluff with almost every unit featuring scintillating views of everything north, south and east of it. The standard rooms are nice, but the three romantic suites are remarkable. "The Saratoga Suite," complete with bay windows, marble fireplace and cozy but posh English furnishings, is phenomenal. Gourmet breakfasts are delivered to every room for a private, leisurely morning meal.

CAFÉ LANGLEY, Whidbey Island

113 First Street, Langley
(206) 221-3090
Inexpensive to Moderate

From the ferry dock follow Highway 525 into Langley. Turn right on Maxwelton Road, then bear left on Langley Road which becomes Cascade which becomes First Street.

I know it seems an unlikely combination — Greek cuisine, Northwest ingredients, a country setting, and romance — but that is exactly what you'll find all under one roof at Café Langley. The menu listings have a definite Greek flare, and the entrees are made with local fresh fish and just-picked produce. The petite interior has white stucco walls, wood-beamed ceilings and terra-cotta tile floors, with only a handful of oak tables and chairs. The service is friendly and attentive, and by the time dessert comes you will be wonderfully pleased with your entire experience. The only drawback is the café's popularity, so you might have to wait for a table.

FRANCISCO'S, Whidbey Island
510 Cascade, Langley
(206) 221-2728
Moderate to Expensive

From the ferry dock follow Highway 525 into Langley. Turn right on Maxwelton Road, then bear left on Langley Road which becomes Cascade. The restaurant will be on the water side of the road.

Francisco's is Langley's newest addition to dining out in supreme island style. This elegant new restaurant has a premium setting on a bluff overlooking Saratoga Passage. The entire blue-grey home is wrapped in beveled-glass windows that take full advantage of the magnificent location. The interior of peach and jade is accented by stained glass windows, very pretty wall sconces and ample seating. The ambience is best described as modern-Victorian, a soft mix of chic and country. Though at the time this book went to press it was still a bit early to report on the consistency of the kitchen, from all appearances, formal dining has arrived in Langley.

◆ *Romantic Warning:* Although smoking is not permitted in the restaurant it is permitted in the adjacent small lounge, which makes for a fairly unbreathable atmosphere in that section of the restaurant.

CLIFF HOUSE, Whidbey Island
5440 Windmill Road, Freeland
(206) 321-1566
Unbelievably Expensive

Take Interstate 5 north from Seattle to Mukilteo. Take the Mukilteo ferry to Clinton on Whidbey Island. Follow Highway 525 for 10.6 miles to Bush

Point Road. Turn left and drive 1.5 miles to Windmill Road, where you turn left again. The road dead-ends; turn right at the brown mailbox and follow the winding driveway down to Cliff House.

Bed & breakfasts, more often than not, are preferable to the run-of-the-mill hotels and motels that line tourist areas all over the Northwest. Cliff House not only triumphs over standard hotels, it alters the entire concept of bed & breakfast establishments. This is a sensuous, architecturally renowned, Northwest contemporary home, where the owner turns the keys over to you for 13 acres of island exclusivity.

The wood-timbered home rests on a towering bluff overlooking Admiralty Inlet where awesome island sunsets seem to be part of the interior floor plan. An outdoor hot tub gives you a steamy perspective on this nightly performance. A glass-enclosed, floor-to-open-sky atrium stands in the center of the house, allowing the elements safely inside the home for your observation. There are stone floors and soft pastel colors throughout, international antiques, a featherbed covered in the softest down comforter, and floor-to-ceiling panoramic windows (we're talking the width and height of the house). There are no interior doors (except on the bathrooms), yet every room has an abundance of privacy; the house simply flows effortlessly from one level to the next. The kitchen is a gourmet's heaven. Cliff House is an island utopia built for two.

◆ **Romantic Alternative:** SEA CLIFF, 5440 Windmill Road, (206) 321-1566 (Moderate) once again proves that the owners of Cliff House have a rare talent for creating remarkable places where you and your special someone can retreat from the world. This gingerbread cottage sits a short distance from Cliff House, on the same bluff with the same premium view. Its private deck is the ideal lounging spot from which to watch the boat traffic navigate its way through Puget Sound. Inside, everything is warmed by a striking stone fireplace, and there is a petite kitchen where continental breakfast delicacies are supplied each day. Furnishings are plush and there's a comfy quilt-covered queen-size bed.

GUEST HOUSE BED & BREAKFAST COTTAGES,
Whidbey Island   ◆◆◆◆

835 East Christenson Road, Greenbank
(206) 678-3115
Moderate to Expensive

From Seattle, take Interstate 5 north to the Mukilteo ferry dock and take the ferry to Clinton. Once on the island, follow Highway 525 for 16 miles to Christenson Road. Visible from the highway on the west side of the road is the yellow farmhouse where the office is located.

This is a place I almost passed up. The unassuming yellow house is only a few feet from the main road, and from that perspective the place looked relatively uninviting and noisy. I have learned from this experience never to pass up anything based solely on its exterior appearance, because the Guest House interior and acreage is more precious than I would have imagined it could be. The idyllic, cozy log cabins and wondrous log home set amongst 25 acres of meadow and forest are some of the most outstanding kissing places I've ever seen.

These authentic log homes are something out of a storybook. Brimming with petite kitchens, fireplaces, oak furniture, stained glass windows, knotty-pine walls, decks, featherbeds, VCRs private spa tubs and skylights—all have an abundance of charm and romantic potential. Your cabin is stocked with breakfast items with all the ingredients fresh and abundant, including eggs from their own chicken coop. As if that weren't enough, there is even an outdoor hot tub and heated swimming pool on the property.

Three of these cottages are small, intimate quarters, but there are also newer units that are amazingly cozy and yet spacious at the same time, with all the amenities. The last unit to describe is a log mansion without comparison anywhere in the Northwest. This capacious home provides the ultimate experience in togetherness. The huge stone fireplace, large soaking tub and a spa tub, antique wonders, floor-to-ceiling windows and full gourmet kitchen are absolutely fabulous. The Guest House boasts a AAA rating and we agree wholeheartedly, though, we think that a four-lips rating conveys far more relevant information.

♦ *Romantic Outing*: One mile north of the Guest House is **WHIDBEY'S GREENBANK FARM**. This is a vineyard par excellence, with a delightful tasting room and pretty picnic grounds. If you can pull yourself away from your log cabin for a few hours, a premium afternoon is here for the sipping. The loganberry wine and liqueur can help provoke some very sweet kissing.

COLONEL CROCKETT FARM INN, Whidbey Island

1012 South Fort Casey Road, Coupeville
(206) 678-3711
Inexpensive to Moderate

From Seattle take Interstate 5 north to Mukilteo and then the ferry to Clinton. Follow Highway 525 for 23 miles. Turn left onto Highway 20. After 1.4 miles turn right onto Wanamaker Road and drive 1.7 miles. Turn left onto South Fort Casey Road for 0.2 mile. Watch carefully for the sign in front and then turn left into the farm's driveway.

As you pull into Colonel Crockett Farm you'll see a massive red barn that has been restored to some of its former glory and heralds the entrance to the inn. As you enter this consummate Victorian country home, you'll be impressed by its invitation to gracious living. The colors, appointments, hand-crafted wood paneling, private baths and loving personal touches combine to assure you a sublime time away from everything except each other. The dining room is a series of small intimate tables that overlook the garden. A supreme breakfast is served here, with sumptuous egg creations and heavenly fresh-baked breads and muffins.

PLEASANT BEACH GRILL AND OYSTER BAR,
Bainbridge Island

4738 Lynnwood Center Road
(206) 842-4347
Expensive

From the Winslow ferry dock, go to the first light and turn left. Head through the town of Winslow and turn right on Madison Street. At the next stoplight turn left on Wyatt. Follow this road as it curves around, then follow the signs to Lynnwood. Watch for the sign indicating the restaurant.

The ferryboat ride from Seattle to Bainbridge Island in and of itself provides a romantic excursion across the Sound, with the majestic Olympic Mountains on the western horizon and the city skyline to the east. Once you dock at this nearby island, a short car trip will complete the experience. Pleasant Beach Grill is an English Tudor-style restaurant, skillfully renovated from what was once an old, secluded mansion, yet the atmosphere and food are a total Northwest experience. You are served in what was formerly the estate's living room. Beautifully arranged about the room are linen-draped tables accented with china and crystal. As formal as this may sound, the mood and pace are relaxed and comfortable; nothing stuffy is to be found here. Attentive hospitality and imaginative, fresh food are the calling card of this establishment. Their half dozen or so exotic oyster concoctions alone are worth a trip.

After dinner you can step down into the restaurant's petite fireside lounge and sink into one of the leather sofas that surround the stone hearth. Snuggling close together, relax as the crackling fire casts its light on the mahogany-paneled room. For an extra treat, when you're both toasty warm, drive down to the bay and watch the twinkling lights of the marine traffic as it passes through the channel.

◆ *Romantic Suggestion:* If an overnight island visit is your desire, there is no better place to escape to than the **BOMBAY HOUSE BED & BREAKFAST**, 8490 N.E. Beck Road, Bainbridge Island, (206) 842-3926 (Inexpensive to Moderate). This stately country mansion resides high on a hill a mile or so from the shore. The rooms are wonderful, some have views and the generous continental breakfasts are scrumptious.

THE BLOEDEL RESERVE, Bainbridge Island

7571 N.E. Dolphin Drive
(206) 842-7631
$4.00 entrance fee

From Seattle take the Winslow ferry to Bainbridge Island and follow Highway 305 to the north end of the island. Turn right on Dolphin Drive which leads to the estate. Call for reservations; access is limited to a specific number of people each day.

There are over 150 acres of meticulously maintained gardens here at Bloedel Reserve, and each one provides a peaceful haven for an afternoon interlude. The Reserve is a place where the artisticc splendor of sculpted plantlife brings pleasure to the senses. There is a bird sanctuary, verdant woods, Japanese gardens, reflecting pool and a dense moss garden here and all of it is divine. As the brochure for the Bloedel Reserve plainly states: "Man's first recorded home was a garden, no sooner known than lost...and we've been trying to return ever since." This might not be Eden, but it may be the next best thing.

SOUND FOOD, Vashon Island

20312 Vashon Way S.W.
(206) 463-3565
Inexpensive to Moderate

From the Vashon ferry dock, drive eight miles along the main road of the island. At the intersection of 240th and Highway 99, look for the restaurant on the east side of the road.

To start a sunny summer evening off right, take the 6 P.M. ferry from

West Seattle at the Fauntleroy ferry dock across to Vashon Island. (This is only a 15-minute trip, so hurry to the bow of the boat and stand watch on the deck to fully enjoy the crossing.) Almost at the opposite end of the island from the ferry dock, Sound Food extends a standing invitation. This is a very special, love-filled, health-aware gourmet restaurant. You'll find the country atmosphere, hospitality, and freshly prepared food a genuine change of pace. After you've taken a leisurely two hours to relish the various subtleties of your meal and indulge in a second helping of fresh-baked bread, a glimpse out the window should reveal the impending sunset. This is the perfect time to drive to **POINT DEFIANCE LOOKOUT.** Continue along the road that brought you to the restaurant until it ends at the water on the south side of the island. Turn right at the dead-end and continue uphill for about two miles. At the top, keep an eye on the west side of the road for the turnoff. The view across the Sound from up here is devastatingly beautiful. What better way to watch a sunset than next to a significant someone, after a marvelous dinner.

> *"In their choice of lovers, both the male and female reveal their essential nature. The type of human being which we prefer reveals the contours of our heart."*
> Jose Ortega y Gasset

SEATTLE AREA

◆ Hotel/Bed & Breakfast Kissing ◆

ALEXIS HOTEL, Seattle
1007 First Avenue
(206) 624-4844
Expensive to Very Expensive

Six blocks south of the Pike Place Market, on First Avenue between Spring and Madison.

The Alexis Hotel is a very sexy, very exclusive, very expensive place to stay in Seattle. For luxurious details and ample space you can't do much better, particularly if you are willing to go the extra mile and reserve one of the suites that has a wood-burning fireplace, spa tub and formal living room. These lavish accommodations are beautifully appointed and comfortable, and the bathrooms are as sensuous as a bathroom can get. There are no crowds milling about at The Alexis; with only 50 rooms, it can feel quite intimate. So order some room service, light the fire, set your shoes out to be shined and get ready for a very select evening.

◆ *Romantic Suggestion:* Whether or not you are staying overnight at the Alexis Hotel, take time to have lunch or dinner at **CAFÉ ALEXIS**. When you enter the restaurant the aroma of exotic flowers combined with the ambrosial creations simmering in the kitchen will be immediately apparent. Once seated, you will notice that the room has a relaxed atmosphere that is also quite elegant and cozy. The glow from the candles placed on each of the 12 tables softly illuminates the room, reflecting brightly off the mirrored back wall. Elegant tapestry wallpaper complements the floral arrangements placed throughout the restaurant.

Soothing classical music plays faintly in the background. The menu lists an array of Northwest specialties, all exceedingly fresh and delectable, served by gentle, unassuming waiters. While the two of you are savoring your meal, be sure to leave room for one of the sinful desserts for which Café Alexis is famous.

THE GASLIGHT INN, Seattle
1727 15th Avenue
(206) 325-3654
Inexpensive

From downtown, take East Denny Way east to Capitol Hill. Continue on Denny until it becomes John and eventually terminates at 15th Avenue East. Turn right on 15th Avenue East and go two blocks. The Gaslight Inn is on the right-hand side of the road.

The Gaslight Inn, located in Capitol Hill's busy 15th Avenue neighborhood, attracts mainly a business clientele that is weary of staying in one of the 500-unit hotels available downtown. There is a total of 10 attractive and striking rooms here, five with private baths. One is filled with Indian artifacts, while another, with its wood-paneled walls and deer head above the bed, has the flavor of a Northwest hunter's library. Two of the rooms have decks that overlook the backyard pool and the East Seattle skyline. None of the rooms are frilly, but each is the product of a high quality renovation. The plaster walls and ceiling in each room are smooth perfection, painted with coat after coat in one of several deep, rich colors until virtually flawless.

It's clear to me that more than the handsome decor attracts the downtown business crowd to this inn; the efficient manner in which things are run and the consistent attention to detail are also major drawing points. The bottom line for The Gaslight Inn is this: if you're conducting business in the Seattle area and you want your lodging to be as gracious as possible, or if you're conducting pleasure in the Seattle area and you want it to be as intriguing as possible, this place fits the bill.

◆ *Romantic Alternative:* **THE SALISBURY HOUSE,** 750 16th Avenue East, (206) 328-8682 (Very Inexpensive to Inexpensive) is located in an old, established neighborhood on Capitol Hill. This inviting turn-of-the-century home provides its guests with a peaceful oasis from the Hill's colorful but sometimes overwhelmingly busy atmosphere. The decor of The Salisbury is simple but charming. The furniture is comfortable and the polished pine floors shine. There are no rooms with private baths (which explains the Very Inexpensive rating), but one of the three bathrooms used to be a bedroom and is quite large. This bed & breakfast is not fancy; the rooms are clean and cozy but not exceptional, yet the gracious innkeepers, the relaxed atmosphere and the reasonable price make it worth checking into.

◆ *Romantic Suggestion:* **JACK'S BISTRO,** 405 15th Avenue East, (206) 324-9625 (Inexpensive) is just around the corner from The Salisbury House. It's open for breakfast, lunch and dinner and has simple but very good food (it's famous among Capitol Hill-area residents for its omelets). The interior of Jack's Bistro has a high ceiling, black-and-white tiled floors and walls, and an outdoor patio. If possible, try to visit Jack's on a Friday evening when there is a piano player who provides velvety, lilting music.

THE HAINSWORTH HOUSE, Seattle
2657 37th S.W.
(206) 938-1020
Inexpensive

From Interstate 5 go west on the West Seattle Freeway. Take the Admiral Way exit and continue on Admiral to the top of the hill. Turn left on Olga. The Hainsworth House is at the intersection of Olga and 37th S.W.

Built in the early nineteenth century, the owners of this mammoth Tudor-style mansion have created an atmosphere of relaxed luxury and comfort. The Victorian decor is impressive but also homey enough to make one feel compelled to curl up on the soft couch in the TV room, open to all guests, and spend a lazy evening watching old Garbo flicks. Only two rooms are set aside as guest chambers — both have Victorian decor, calico floral prints strewn about, private decks and private baths. The larger room is by far the nicer, with a fireplace, king-size bed, and an outstanding view of downtown Seattle from the deck on a summer evening or through the large bay windows on a cloudy but cozy Northwest day. The smaller room has a spacious deck overlooking the garden. Regardless of the weather, the ever-changing Puget Sound offers the ultimate in soothing scenery. In the morning you wake to a formal gourmet champagne breakfast.

INN AT THE MARKET, Seattle
86 Pine Street
(206) 443-3600
Moderate to Expensive

Located in the Pike Street Market area, at the corner of First and Pike.

To many, the most romantic settings in Seattle are the Pike Place Market and the waterfront, with the Olympics serving as backdrop to both. On your first visit to Seattle you may enjoy a stay right in the center of town, and you can do so in style at Inn at the Market. Although the room decorations are fairly plain, each room has nice touches like large armoires, French country furnishings and excellent service. (There is no morning breakfast served here.)

For those who want proximity to the best of Seattle's landmarks, there's no place like this one.

◆ *Romantic Must:* **CAMPAGNE**, 86 Pine Street, (206) 728-2800 (Expensive), is situated ideally in the courtyard of the Inn at the Market. The food at lunch and dinner is superb, with a creative menu that will satisfy even the must distinguished gourmet. In summer there is outdoor seating in the courtyard, and at night candles flicker against the dreamy, dim lighting.

FOUR SEASONS OLYMPIC HOTEL, Seattle
411 University Street
(206) 6214-1700
Expensive to Unbelievably Expensive

On University between Fourth and Fifth Avenues.

This is one outrageously sexy, ultra-posh downtown Seattle hotel. There are over 400 rooms in this luxuriously renovated landmark building, which is located near everything the city has to offer. The rooms (some with separate sitting parlors) are graciously decorated, but they are still just nice hotel rooms. They won't spark romance in and of themselves. What will sweep you away, though, are the restaurants, health club and lobby area which are all simply sensational. Once you arrive at The Four Seasons you'll have no reason to go anywhere else to fulfill your amorous requirements. While you're enjoying the complimentary health club — a lap-swimming pool, a 20-person spa tub (which seems hardly to be used), a modest workout room and an outdoor lounge — you can arrange for poolside service of fresh coffee and eggs Florentine.

For every other meal, **THE GARDEN COURT** is a radiant composite of tearoom, lounge/bistro and weekend ballroom. It is an immense hall, arrayed with a bevy of trees, marble floors, 40-foot-tall luminous windows, a petite waterfall cascading into a marble pond, and well-spaced groupings of settees, cushioned chairs and glass coffee tables. This prodigious dining room changes appearance as the day progresses: morning espresso, savory lunch, authentic afternoon tea service, evening cocktails, and late-evening, big-band dancing every Friday and Saturday night.

THE GEORGIAN COURT is the very grand, very civilized, very distinguished dining room of the hotel, overflowing with crystal chandeliers, monumental floral arrangements, and subdued lighting. Service includes a very posh breakfast and lunch and a consummate five-star dinner. The cuisine is continental, with an emphasis on presentation and kid-glove service. When you talk about a grand stay in

Seattle, you're talking about The Four Seasons Olympic.

◆ **Romantic Note:** Ask the hotel about its specially priced romantic weekend packages.

LAKE UNION BED & BREAKFAST, Seattle
2217 North 36th Street
(206) 547-9965
Moderate to Expensive

Call for reservations and directions.

I must caution you about two problems with this bed & breakfast: first, even if you have good directions and know Seattle, the home is a trick to find (so be sure to ask for *very* specific directions); second, when you do finally locate the address and walk inside, you'll want the owners to move out so you can move in. This is an impressive, three-story wood home overlooking the north end of Lake Union. You enter through a landscaped garden enclosed by a six-foot-tall brick wall. The modest-size interior has thick white carpeting, interesting art pieces and overstuffed white chairs flanking a marble fireplace. Hors d'oeuvres and a prize-winning wine or champagne laced with Chambord liqueur await your sampling on arrival.

The house can accommodate two couples. The penthouse is a huge room adorned by willow furniture and a fireplace of brown marble. The bathroom has a large spa tub with a superb view of the lake and city, and there are control-heated tile floors that flow into the sun-drenched solarium, which has the same wonderful view. The other upstairs bedroom, which is much less expensive, is simple and comfortable and has a private bathroom located down on the main floor. That would automatically be a romantic no-no if the bathroom didn't contain a glass-brick-enclosed sauna, piped-in music and a large tiled shower. Oh yes, and the breakfast: a superlative seven-course culinary presentation of souffles, pastries, lattes, fruits, granola, egg dishes and anything else the owner/chef creates, served on Lenox china and Baccarat crystal.

This is one of the absolutely best places to kiss in Seattle, whether you're eating, sleeping, standing, or lounging.

◆ *Romantic Note:* Upon request, the eccentric and brilliant owner/ chef of the house, who has a Type-A personality, will prepare a dinner feast for you at the bed & breakfast. You can also partake of her gourmet skills at her restaurant, **TEGER'S**, 2302 24th Avenue East, Seattle, (206) 324-3373 (Moderate). The restaurant is open just Wednesday through Saturday (one seating only), and then only when the chef is in town. For an extra-intimate touch, call Teger's ahead of time and describe the meal of your dreams and it can be served to you that evening; or, on the nights when the restaurant is closed, you may make the same request at the bed & breakfast, whether or not you're spending the night.

◆ *Romantic Alternative:* When you drive up to **THE QUEEN ANNE HILL BED AND BREAKFAST**, 1835 Seventh West, (206) 284-9779 (Very Inexpensive to Inexpensive), you're likely to wonder if you've come to the right place. There is no sign and the house address is difficult to make out through the profusion of flora that engulfs the pathway. Yet if you're bold enough to wade through the forest of groping cosmos and daisies, the awesome view is yet another example of the Northwest's abundant beauty. While eating a healthy and natural breakfast in the dining room or out on the deck, you are treated to a sweeping view of Puget Sound, Magnolia, and West Seattle. There are a total of three rooms here that are funky but comfortable. The rooms have double beds, two have awesome views of the Sound, but only one has a private bath. The shared bath, however, is large and decorated with Victorian lace and detailing. While The Queen Anne Bed & Breakfast definitely has its problems — dated brown carpet, threadbare Oriental rugs, and a decor that is a bit too eclectic, its rare panoramic view can compensate for these faults.

THE SORRENTO HOTEL, Seattle
900 Madison Street
(206) 622-6400
Expensive to Unbelievably Expensive

At Madison and Terry streets, about six blocks east of downtown Seattle.

Generally, you can assume that downtown hotels are designed to handle large groups of people efficiently — conventioneers, business executives and tourists — with the basic conveniences of bar, restaurant and gift shop. They exist solely to facilitate quick check-ins and quick departures. But every now and then there is an exception to the rule — a smaller high-scale renovation where the mood is intimate and tranquil and the attention very personal. The Sorrento is such a hotel.

The **FIRESIDE ROOM** next to the lobby is a handsome, albeit formal, assortment of settees, sofas and chairs wrapping around an imposing hand-painted tile-and-stone fireplace. It is wonderfully inviting for an early-evening conversation or an after-dinner aperitif. The restaurant here is called **THE HUNT CLUB**. It is a seductively lit (bordering on dark) dining room with Honduran-mahogany paneling framing brick walls. The service is almost too attentive, but the food is creative and carefully prepared. Your every need will be obligingly met, including privacy — even the waiters will have trouble seeing you. With its lobby bar and The Hunt Club, The Sorrento bears no resemblance to a typical hotel.

◆ Restaurant Kissing ◆

AL BOCCALINO, Seattle   ◖◗◖◗
1 Yesler Way
(206) 622-7688
Inexpensive to Moderate

From downtown, go south on First Avenue to Pioneer Square. Turn right on Yesler. Al Boccalino is on the left side of the street at the very end of Yesler Way.

This tiny brick-walled restaurant is located in a vintage building that is typical of many in the Pioneer Square area. The interior is both formal and homey. Floral curtains are strung across the middle of wrought-iron-caged windows. The floor is covered with an institutional green tile with multicolored flecks that reminds me of my elementary school hallway. In contrast, the white tablecloths are starched to perfection, and dignified turn-of-the-century lamps hang from the ceiling and shed soft light throughout the restaurant. The hodge-podge becomes charming the instant you pick up the menu. Classic and unusual Italian dishes are offered here. If you're looking for some of the city's finest Italian cuisine and a subdued, intimate, neighborhood atmosphere, Al Boccalino should be first on your list.

THE B & O ESPRESSO — See Hamilton Viewpoint
(Outdoor Kissing)

THE BYZANTION, Seattle
806 East Roy
(206) 325-7580
Inexpensive to Moderate

Take Broadway Street north through the Capitol Hill district to East Roy

Street and turn west. The Byzantion is on the north side of the street, across from the Harvard Exit movie theatre.

Seattle's Broadway district is no match for its New York namesake, yet this promenade of boutiques, cafés and restaurants is a magnet for almost every lifestyle. A half-mile walk down this street of glitzy variety can be fun and educational for anyone in the mood to browse the shops and watch the people. After you've had your fill, duck onto East Roy at the north end of Broadway. Hidden there, away from all the madness, is this demure, cozy Greek restaurant that promotes intimate dining. The room is awash in low, golden light regardless of the time of day. Russian murals in soft, earthen tones cover the walls. The cuisine is mostly traditional Greek and remarkably tasty, including several vegetarian dishes. The staff is patient and unusually considerate.

◆ *Romantic Note:* The restaurant serves a health-aware breakfast and Sunday brunch of whole-wheat pancakes and waffles, with fresh-roasted coffee and fresh-squeezed juices.

CAFÉ DILETTANTE, Seattle

1600 Post Alley
(206) 728-9144 or
416 Broadway East
(206) 329-6463
Inexpensive

In the Pike Place Market, on Stewart Street, or on Broadway Street, between Republican and Harrison.

All right, I admit it, I'm a chocolate lover, and even if this place weren't charming I'd still be a fan. The Dilettante's chocolates are the stuff of dreams (and outrageous temptations to excess). Café Dilettante on Capitol Hill has charming wood tables and a dimly lit chocolatey-brown interior, and the one downtown in the Market has marble tabletops arced around a glass showcase of creamy morsels. The Capitol Hill location is actually the more romantic in design, but the crowds here often interrupt the mood. This is particularly regrettable in the evening, when sharing a torte covered in *ephemere* sauce is the only way to say goodnight — except for a kiss, that is. The café in the Market is, for some unknown reason, rarely full and as a result is always romantic.

CAFÉ SOPHIE, Seattle
1921 First Avenue
(206) 441-6139
Inexpensive to Moderate

Café Sophie is located in downtown Seattle, about half a block north of the Pike Place Market, between Stewart and Virginia.

The owner of Café Sophie has quietly managed it so that sophisticated elegance coexists here with romantic coziness and comfort. The restaurant's high gold-trimmed ceilings and starched white linen tablecloths are softened by the inviting forest-green color scheme. The walls are covered with gold-leaf mirrors that reflect glowing light from delicate lamps on each table. One wall of the restaurant is lined with booths framed by rich green, gold-tasseled curtains. In back there's a room called The Library, which is worth requesting when making reservations because it has a sweeping view of Puget Sound. In addition, the fireplace, burgundy velvet seats, tapestry cushions and book-lined shelves make comfort and elegance the closest of companions. As if this ideal atmosphere weren't enough, the food is truly superior — soups with unique Northwest seasonings, and fresh pastas and seafood are prepared with the utmost of care. What's more, Café Sophie has the best desserts in Seattle. That alone warrants your serious consideration.

CAMPAGNE — See Inn at the Market (Hotel/B&B Kissing)

CHEZ SHEA, Seattle
94 Pike Street #34
(206) 467-9990
Moderate to Expensive

Chez Shea is located in the upstairs of a Pike Place Market building that houses Left Bank Books, on the corner of First and Pike.

At night, after you've walked through the deserted Market and quietly watched the sky turn from vivid blue to glowing crimson, you can climb the wooden stairs that lead to Chez Shea and share an unforgettable gourmet dinner. The restaurant is small, so any table affords a view of Puget Sound and West Seattle, but if possible, try to sit near one of the arched windows so that you can also look down on the happenings in the street below.

This restaurant's dark wood floors, creamy cinnamon-colored walls, white arched windows, high ceilings and period character set the stage for the ultimate romantic evening. The menu at Chez Shea features five different five-course meals. The food is French and creatively prepared each night: roulade of prosciutto, figs, stilton and goat cheese with a port glaze, scallops in champagne sauce served in a potato basket, and blackberry mousse are just a few examples. This is the perfect place to take someone special if you both love the Market and want a dinner ambience oozing with character and charm.

IL TERRAZZO CARMINE, Seattle
411 First Avenue South
(206) 467-7797
Expensive

In Seattle's Pioneer Square, on First Avenue between Jackson and King Streets.

Il Terrazzo Carmine is a poetic city nightspot, right in the middle of what is not the prettiest part of Pioneer Square. You'll enter through a brick archway where a ceramic aqua-blue-tiled fountain cascades into a series of spotlighted ponds. Strategically placed backlighting reflects off the water and makes the patio shimmer and gleam in the night air. This is the restaurant's backyard, where tables are set during the summer. Inside there is even more evidence of romantic detail in the pretty dining room, replete with comfortable rattan chairs, crystal, and floral-patterned china, all arranged to encourage close encounters.

Rest assured that the food is also an essential part of the atmosphere. The kitchen consistently prepares a combination of traditional and daring Italian dishes, with an exceptional antipasto presentation. Your evening can easily be centered around the al dente food and glowing ambience of Il Terrazzo Carmine.

JACK'S BISTRO — See Gaslight Inn (Hotel/B&B Kissing)

LA DOLCE VITA, Seattle
3426 N.E. 55th Street
(206) 523-3313
Moderate

At the intersection of 35th Avenue N.E. and N.E. 55th Street.

This engaging restaurant is as authentically Italian as it is thoroughly amorous. Terra-cotta-tiled floors, soft lighting from wrought iron chandeliers, Romanesque-style art and wall hangings, floor-to-ceiling windows and well-spaced seating are all part of the warm, attractive setting. Hearty, deftly prepared and perfectly seasoned pastas, meat and fish dishes are served here. Every bite is a flavorful sensation. The very Italian owners bring a joyous, friendly atmosphere to the elegant surroundings, and this combination makes for one of the most wonderful dining experiences we've ever had in Seattle.

MAXIMILIEN-IN-THE-MARKET, Seattle

814 Pike Street
(206) 682-7270
Inexpensive to Moderate

In the Pike Place Market, at the south end of the arcade, facing the water. Look for the entrance in the area of shops to the left of the clock.

I am always searching for the quintessential romantic breakfast place. At Maximilien's there's a relaxed atmosphere at all meals, but especially at breakfast. This modest restaurant, with a small array of wood tables, walls covered with antique mirrors, and a mesmerizing view of the Sound and Olympics, serves a very French and usually tasty morning meal. Souffles, eggs Benedict, shirred eggs and fresh pastries are the daily selections, and Sunday brunch adds a few standard lunch selections. Maximilien's also serves a good French dinner that is reasonably priced and features the Olympics changing color in harmony with the setting sun.

Having said all that, I hate to report that the service can be slow, the portions small and the kitchen, on occasion, fails in getting things quite right. Shirred eggs are not supposed to be poached, and a brioche should be full and puffy, not bent over and deflated. Everything still tastes good, but with a little more effort it could be better.

◆ *Romantic Alternative:* **THE OTHER PLACE**, 96 Union Street, Seattle, (206) 623-7340 (Moderate to Expensive) is located in downtown Seattle near the Pike Place Market. While the interior of this restaurant is not exceptionally romantic (it's very handsome and perfect for a business lunch), the outside deck has a view of Puget Sound that is hard to beat. For this reason, the best time to dine at The Other Place is during the summer months when the deck is open and you can seek refuge from the madness of First Avenue. The majority of the menu items are seafood and pasta, served with gourmet sauces and relishes that will please even the most particular of palates.

THE MIRABEAU RESTAURANT, Seattle
1001 Fourth Avenue
(206) 624-4550
Expensive

*In downtown Seattle on the 46th floor of the 1001 Fourth Avenue Plaza
Building, at the intersection of Fourth Avenue and Madison Street.*

Most of the dinner crowd in Seattle, particularly those who have been
dining out in the area for some time, will be surprised to see The
Mirabeau listed as a best kissing place. It is a vintage restaurant, and
though it has always been known for its reliable kitchen, it has also been
known for being a bit stuffy. But no more. Today a new, softer pastel
interior erases all of that stuffiness and the view is still glorious, resulting
in one of Seattle's more notable places for a pleasurable meal or dessert.
From the 46th floor, facing Puget Sound, you'll feel that you are soaring
over the Olympics, the Sound and the broad cityscape. Rosy orange
sunsets fill the western sky and set the mountains in dark relief. As the
sunset fades, a dance of lights from the darkening buildings below
enlivens the city night. This setting — combined with perfectly cooked
salmon, piquant sauces, and the one you love — is absolutely splendid
for romance.

QUEEN MARY CONFECTIONERS, Seattle
2912 N.E. 55th Street
(206) 527-2770
Inexpensive

On N.E. 55th Street between 29th and 30th Avenues N.E.

It is easy to drive past this small storefront restaurant, though it is
probably the most romantic restaurant in Seattle. Once inside you will
feel as if you've been transported to the English countryside. This
exceedingly charming, polished restaurant has a beautiful interior of
wood paneling, pleated floral fabric lining the walls and entrance,

English-lace-covered windows, and comfortable wicker chairs placed around a handful of tables set for two. Fastidious attention to detail and freshness is to be found here at every meal. Breakfast is an elaborate display of fresh pastries, granolas and breads; midday brings light, flaky quiches and generous sandwiches; and dinner is an elegant gourmet event. Roast leg of lamb stuffed with red and yellow peppers, and pasta with artichokes and smoked salmon in a heavenly cream sauce were both sumptuous. High tea is also part of the daily offerings and you will be properly impressed with this procession too. But I've left the best for last — dessert. The most outrageous, luscious cakes, tortes and mousses are made fresh here daily. Chocolate cake with Amaretto mousse, marbled cheesecake and fresh fruit tarts were only a few of the selections available the night we fell in love with Queen Mary.

ROVER'S

2808 East Madison
(206) 325-7442
Moderate to Expensive

At the corner of Madison and 28th Street.

An unassuming neighborhood setting, a discreet interior, subtly dramatic lighting, white walls covered with pastel art and some of the most sumptuous continental cuisine you will ever taste is what you will find at Rover's. Perhaps the decor is a bit stark to be considered cozy or charming, but sophisticated, elegant dining is also an enticing calling card for a personal celebration. The chef here has incredible skill and it is demonstrated in dishes like quenelles of salmon with tomato fondue in a dry vermouth sauce, filo dough filled with goat cheese, tomato concasse with a goat cheese sauce, steamed lobster with a black truffle sauce and rabbit served with caramelized garlic and huckleberry sauce. Outstanding!

TEGER'S — See Lake Union Bed & Breakfast (Hotel Kissing)

◆ Outdoor Kissing ◆

"BHY" KRACKE PARK

Take Fifth Avenue North from downtown to Highland Drive on southeast Queen Anne Hill. The park is at the intersection of Fifth Avenue North and Highland. It is also known as Comstock Park.

Unless you have read the original version of *The Best Places To Kiss*, or live in this neighborhood, you probably don't know that this park with the funny name even exists. As you drive through the unpretentious neighborhood, you'll probably think nothing of the small unobtrusive playground on your left. But wait, stop and take another look. "Bhy" Kracke Park starts off as an innocent playground, less than a block long, at the bottom of a hill. On either side of it landscaped walkways begin angling upwards, meet, curve around and up, and around and up, to the top of the hill. As you follow the course upward you will find five tiers of grassy vistas, park benches surrounded by dense hedges and vines — all pointing toward a startling city view. Around each turn is another glimpse of the city, creating a build-up for what lies at the top. When you get there you'll exclaim, "This is unbelievable!"

◆ *Romantic Note:* If you don't want to walk up, drive to the entrance on Comstock at the top of the hill and walk down one tier.

DISCOVERY PARK SAND CLIFFS, Seattle

The park is in northwest Magnolia. To enter the park from Magnolia Boulevard, take the Magnolia Bridge exit off Elliott Avenue and stay to your left. At the first stop sign, turn left onto Magnolia Boulevard and follow it till it dead-ends at the park's southeast entrance.

Discovery Park is an unusual area with an amazing variety of trails and terrain. You can hike through dense woods or along sandy cliffs above Puget Sound where there's unmarred exposure to everything due north, south and west. Or take the wooden steps leading down to the shore and ramble over driftwood, rocky shoreline and sandy beach. While wandering through your new romantic discovery (pun intended), look for the sand cliffs on the southwest side of the park. During the winter, when sundown occurs in the late afternoon, come stand atop these golden dunes for an intoxicating view of day passing into night.

◆ *Romantic Note:* **MAGNOLIA BOULEVARD** snakes around the edge of the Magnolia area of Seattle on the way to Discovery Park. This urban borough is blessed by a majestic 180-degree view of the Sound. The cliffs along its southwest border showcase the city and the Olympics. As you follow the drive, you will notice several obvious places to pull off and park. The panoramas from these areas are spectacular but, unfortunately, no privacy is afforded there. However, if you walk from the grass-lined curb down to the edge of the cliff overlooking the water, the street is no longer visible. A wool blanket will help make the damp grass more comfortable.

HAMILTON VIEWPOINT, West Seattle

Take Interstate 5 to the West Seattle Freeway exit and the West Seattle Bridge. Cross the bridge and follow Admiral Way Southwest to California Street. Turn right and stay on California to the viewpoint.

The waterfront neighborhoods of West Seattle are only a few minutes from downtown. The areas along Alki Beach and Lincoln Park look out to the west, and the east-side area faces the city; both are bustling places during the summer. During the fall and winter, when things quiet down, these are blissful areas to stroll and watch the sky and city change expressions with the passing hours. Hamilton Viewpoint is a nicely designed turnoff that faces the downtown skyline of Seattle. From here you can watch the reflections of the buildings' twinkling lights in the cobalt-blue water and the moon's golden glow over the surface. This is also a rare vantage point from which to watch sunrise above Seattle. Of course you won't be the only couple embracing in the moonlight, but you will probably be the only ones snuggling in the early light of dawn.

◆ **Romantic Note:** The B & O Café on Capitol Hill is not a place one would go for an intimate encounter — an encounter with the '60s maybe, but not with romance. But the **B & O ESPRESSO**, 2352 California Avenue S.W., (206) 935-1540 (Inexpensive) in West Seattle is exceptionally romantic and one of the most inviting places to stop for a latte and a rich death-by-chocolate dessert. Jade green columns, small wrought iron tables, marble tabletops, lofty ceiling, pretty wall sconces and subdued lighting create a lovely, warm setting.

HIGHLAND DRIVE, Seattle

From Roy Street in Queen Anne, turn onto the steep part of Queen Anne Avenue North. Two blocks up, turn left on West Highland Drive and follow it along the southwestern slope of the hill.

This exclusive street, lined with mansions and classic older apartment buildings, has a prominent southwestern view from below the summit of Queen Anne Hill. When you reach the intersection of Seventh Avenue West, Eighth Place West and West Highland, you will have discovered a grand panoramic vista. There is a grassy knoll up here with benches from which you'll have the most sweeping, complete view of the city skyline and the Olympic Mountains. With a picnic basket in tow, you can spend an entire summer afternoon up here in each other's arms.

HOT-AIR BALLOONING

There are several balloon companies in the Seattle area and in other areas of the Northwest and Southwest Canada. Check the Yellow Pages for the one nearest you.

If you're thinking that a hot-air balloon ride sounds like a frivolous, expensive, childish sort of excursion, you're right. It is a Mary Poppins liftoff into fantasy-land. After an evening balloon ride, the term "carried away" will suddenly have new meaning.

Usually you depart just before sunset. Your first impression will be astonishment at the enormous mass of billowing material overhead and the dragon fire that fills it with air. As you step into the gondola your heart will begin to flutter with expectation. Once aloft, as the wind guides your craft above the countryside, the world will seem more peaceful than you ever thought possible. You will also be startled at the splendor of sunset from way up here as twilight covers the mountains with muted color and warmth. A caress while floating over the world on a cloudless summer evening can be a thoroughly heavenly experience.

◆ *Romantic Note:* Some balloon companies provide champagne and pastries after your flight.

WATERFALL GARDEN, Seattle

Just north of the Kingdome, at the northwest corner of Washington and Main Streets. The park closes around 9 P.M.

United Parcel Service built this lush urban garden as a gift to the citizens of Seattle, and it is a unique city hideaway. This cloistered downtown oasis is enclosed by stone walls and a wrought-iron gate. A large rushing waterfall tumbles over boulders at the back of the garden, its pleasantly noisy rush helping to drown out any evidence that civilization is right next door. There are tables and chairs here which make it a convenient place for a refreshing afternoon picnic. You can also use the garden for a rendezvous with someone special before a football game, dinner, or theatre. Except at lunchtime, you're likely to be quite alone together here.

◆ Worth The Trip ◆

CHATEAU SAINTE MICHELLE WINERY   ❤❤❤
Woodinville

1411 N.E. 145th
(206) 488-1133

From Interstate 405 North or South, take the Wenatchee/Monroe exit. Follow Highway 522 East and take the Woodinville exit. Keep right and at the second stoplight turn right onto 175th. At the four-way stop, turn left onto Highway 202. Go two miles to the winery, which is on the left-hand side.

Built in the style of a French country chateau, this well-known winery offers more than superior Northwest wines to its visitors. The 87 acres of manicured grounds are ideal for lazy strolls, complimentary wine tastings and daily cellar tours, particularly during the fall harvesting season. There is also a summer-long series of performances, ranging from jazz to Shakespeare, in the outdoor amphitheater. The winery's giftstore offers meats, cheeses, exquisite wines and truffles — all the essentials for the perfect picnic.

IDYL INN, Carnation   ❤

4548 Tolt River Road
(206) 333-4262
Inexpensive to Expensive

Call for reservations and directions.

Idyl Inn is located in Carnation on a seven-acre organic hobby farm. This contemporary home rests on a secluded lot near the shores of the Tolt River. While the town of Carnation is not the first place you'd think to come for a romantic exploit, Idyl Inn provides its guests with a multitude of relaxing activities and a serene, restful atmosphere. The indoor solar-heated pool, sauna, hot tub, and outdoor patio are ideal for two lovers interested in a healthy hideaway. There are three rooms here, two of which are fairly small, share a bathroom, and are plainly decorated. The third room is the only room I recommend. While not elegant, it has all the amenities you need — a refrigerator filled with fresh juices and mineral water, thick terrycloth robes, coffee maker, king-size bed, and a shower big enough to be a fourth room. The bed is covered in a creamy lace spread that complements the mauve and soft rose color scheme. When you look out the window you see the Tolt River rushing by (of course, how much it's rushing depends on the time of year) and the organic hobby farm, which looks more like an unkempt garden.

THE SALISH LODGE, Snoqualmie   ❖
37807 S.E. Fall City Snoqualmie Road
(206) 888-2556
Expensive to Very Expensive

From Interstate 90 going east from Seattle, take the Snoqualmie Falls Exit (Highway 202) and follow the signs to the lodge at the head of the falls.

The Salish Lodge has almost everything going for it: a well-respected name, a celebrated Northwest location at the head of Snoqualmie Falls, and outstanding, thoroughly romantic accommodations. Each of the guestrooms has a plush, country decor with furnishings that ooze comfort and invite tenderness. Plus each room has a spa tub and a well-stocked wood-burning fireplace. The popular dining room here is elegantly appointed, with views of the falls from almost every seat.

You'll have noticed that I said this place has *almost* everything. What it lacks is a Northwest attitude and a kitchen that knows what it's doing. The staff at the front desk and in the restaurant seem to be constantly impatient and somewhat annoyed. Perhaps that's due to the throngs of tourists that must barrage them with questions day in and day out. The food is passable, but just barely — and that's really disappointing given the number of people who eat here daily, particularly on weekends. The other disappointment is that only a handful of the rooms have views of the falls; the rest look out to the road or the power plant upstream.

I guess you'll have to decide this one for yourselves. I can't make up my mind.

THE HERBFARM, Fall City ❂❂❂❀
32804 Issaquah-Fall City Road
(206) 784-2222
Moderate

Call for reservations and directions.

I almost didn't include this restaurant entry because reservations are practically impossible to obtain. Bookings for the fall/winter season are taken during the last week in August and are snatched up immediately through January; summer reservations are taken the third week in April and the entire season is full by the end of the first day. Now if that doesn't whet your curiosity and appetite, I don't know what will.

This farm restaurant, set in the middle of a forested suburban neighborhood, is home to some of the most exotic Northwest cuisine you will ever taste. Part restaurant, part herb garden, part gift and plant shop — the main theme here is reverence toward the earth and sustenance of life. The small, charming dining room with skylights and open kitchen serves delectable concoctions such as a parfait mousse of wild mushroom, king salmon in a zucchini blossom, herb sorbets and rosemary shortbread cookies. The interior is a bit eccentric, but adorable. If you are lucky enough to get a reservation, dinner for two here is more than just romantic, it's irresistible.

DOWNEY HOUSE BED & BREAKFAST &   ◗◖
BLACKBERRY PIE, La Conner

1880 Chilberg Road
(206) 466-3207
Inexpensive to Moderate

From Interstate 5 heading north from Seattle, take exit #221 west onto Fir
Island Road. This will curve north and become Chilberg Road. The house is
on the west side of the road.

If this place weren't located on the main road into La Conner, I would
give it a four-lips rating, because it's an impeccable place to spend
cherished moments together. But this thoroughfare can be fairly busy
and even more so in the summer and on weekends. All the rooms in this
renovated Victorian farmhouse are country beautiful, with private
baths, ample space, tremendously comfortable beds and soothing details,
which include the blackberry pie mentioned in the name. This early-
evening treat is a mouth-watering mound of berries lovingly placed
between the lightest crusts possible, and topped with a scoop of slowly
melting vanilla ice cream. The best room is the suite attached to the
garage, where everything is a lush forest green and the entrance is
private. (At this writing the hot tub in back is broken, which disappointed
us, but not enough to significantly affect our enjoyable stay here.)

◆ *Romantic Alternative:* **RAINBOW INN**, 1075 Chilberg Road,
(206) 466-4578 (Inexpensive to Moderate), much like Downey House,
is an impressively renovated Victorian farmhouse set too close to the
main road. The saving graces here are the yellow blooms of mustard
plants that flank the home and the sweeping view over the valley to
Mount Baker. There are three floors of country-rustic rooms, most of
which have pleasant views of the valley, though the preferred choices
are the ones with private bath. (The shared baths are not the best.) In
the morning a hearty breakfast is served in a charming enclosed sundeck
lined with tables set for two.

THE HERON, La Conner
117 Maple Street
(206) 466-4626
Inexpensive to Moderate

From Interstate 5 heading north from Seattle, take exit #221 west onto Fir Island Road. This will curve north and become Chilberg Road. As you approach the town of La Conner, look for Maple Street and turn left to the inn.

This inn was built to perfection. Each room, even the inexpensive ones, is a warm, pleasing place in which to cuddle when you decide to escape the crowds during the local Tulip Festival or the flocks of summer visitors in the shops in town. The Heron is intended to be a Victorian-style inn, though the exterior is a bit too modern-looking to be convincing. But inside, the rooms are filled with antique furnishings, wood-framed beds, beamed ceilings and thick down comforters. All have private baths and some have spa tubs, views and fireplaces. The outdoor hot tub is also part of the lure. A continental breakfast is served in the formal dining room, though you are free to take yours up to the privacy of your room or out on any of the three back decks.

SCHNAUZER CROSSING, Bellingham
4421 Lakeway Drive
(206) 733-0055
Inexpensive to Moderate

From Interstate 5 heading north from Everett, take the Lakeway Drive exit east for 3 miles and then turn left onto Lakeway Drive. Watch for the signs that lead to the house.

With all due apologies to those who may feel insulted, I do not consider Bellingham to be a romantic destination. But there are two places nearby that offer good reasons to visit the area: the wonderfully renovated Fairhaven District, and the intriguing start of Chuckanut

Drive. Furthermore, the spellbinding slopes of Mount Baker are only an hour's drive to the east.

While you're in the Bellingham area taking advantage of these select sites, Schnauzer Crossing more then meets the criteria of an intimate getaway. Set on a bluff overlooking Lake Whatcom, this contemporary home with wood-beamed cathedral ceilings, floor-to-ceiling windows and sweeping lawns, is a bed & breakfast dream come true. The Master Suite looks like a small apartment. It has a private entrance through a tree-framed garden, a king-size bed, an alcove sitting area, stereo, wood-burning fireplace, and a huge bathroom with a sizable spa tub and roomy double-head shower. Believe me, you will step into this suite and not want to leave. The other room is nice and comfortable, with its own bath, terrycloth robes and views of the lake, but it doesn't compare to the Master Suite. Breakfast is a lavish presentation of gourmet delights that the innkeepers take great pride in preparing. If you can pull yourselves away from your room, venture down to the lake for some sailing, canoeing, fishing or swimming, and afterwards you can take a good long steamy soak in the outdoor hot tub.

IL FIASCO

1309 Commercial Street
(206) 676-9136
Moderate to Expensive

On Commercial between Holly and Magnolia.

Il Fiasco is Bellingham's premier dining location and it lives up to its reputation nightly. The becoming interior of brick walls, wood tables and exposed heating ducts is a polished atmosphere in which to savor some outstanding Italian creations. Your attentive waitperson and the accomplished kitchen staff will help make your meal a special event. The four-cheese lasagne in a garlic cream sauce was as rich and delicious as it sounds, and the pasta with garlic, sun-dried tomatoes, and artichokes mixed with fresh tuna and salmon was flawless. Romance may not be the primary reason to come to Il Fiasco, but after you eat a superlative meal here, that's surely what will happen.

CHUCKANUT DRIVE

Between La Conner and Bellingham, hugging the coast almost the entire way. From Interstate 5 just south of Bellingham, take the Old Fairhaven Parkway exit west about a mile, where it intersects with Chuckanut Drive.

The visual delights of this landmark coastal drive begin almost the minute you start your journey. If you're heading south, the exhibition starts with forested cliffs that reach down to water's edge. At the horizon lies the silhouette of Lummi Island, and in the distance the rugged coastline of Chuckanut Bay. As you continue south the varying patterns of islands, forest and meadows form a panorama. **LARRABEE STATE PARK**, eight miles outside of Bellingham, is a wonderful place to stop and walk along the chiseled beach and see the sights up close.

◆ *Romantic Note:* Approximately 30 minutes outside of Bellingham, about halfway through your Chuckanut Drive excursion, you will come to two culinary mileposts. The renowned **OYSTER BAR**, 240 Chuckanut Drive, (206) 766-6185 (Expensive) has endured 70 years and is more then ever a cozy spot for Northwest gourmet dining with an outstanding view of Samish Bay. **THE OYSTER CREEK INN**, 190 Chuckanut Drive, (206) 766-6179 (Moderate) is enveloped by forest, just a minute's drive north of The Oyster Bar. The interior is all wood with nautical accents and the mood is casual and unhurried. Everything on the menu is classic Northwest seafood with all the fixings, including friendly service. Either place provides a serene, inviting atmosphere for lunch or dinner.

> "Madam, it is the hardest thing in the world
> to be in love, and yet attend to business.
> A gentleman asked me this morning,
> "What news from Lisbon," and I answered,
> "She is exquisitely handsome."
>
> Sir Richard Steele

Washington Cascades

The Washington Cascade Range is spectacular. To the north, Mount Baker's glacial peak stands guard near the Canadian-U.S. border. South from Mount Baker for 200 miles lie mesmerizing scenery and wilderness including national forests, parks and mountain passes, with startling views of the volcanic giants: Mount Rainier, Mount St. Helens and Mount Adams. This chain of mountains, patterned with old-growth evergreens, snow-covered cliffs and countless plummeting waterfalls and spirited rivers culminates at the deep-cut Columbia River Gorge at Vantage. In whichever direction you travel in this area, you will encounter radically different landscapes, climates and colors. In contrast to the wet, vivid greenery on the west side of the Cascades, the east side of the mountains is authentic Marlboro country — awash in hues of gold, bathed in hot sunshine in summer and snowy cold in winter. Almost every square foot of this expanse is magnificent.

The most popular and accessible route through the region is the **CASCADE LOOP**, a series of connecting highways through the northern section of the mountains. The Loop starts just south of Everett, where Highway 2 heads east across Stevens Pass to the town of Leavenworth on the east side of the mountains. Just before Wenatchee, take Highway 97 north to Chelan where you continue heading north on Highway 153 toward the towns of Twisp and Winthrop. From here you take Highway 20 west again toward Mazama, back across the Cascades to Interstate 5. The Loop continues out to La Conner and down through Whidbey Island, finishing with a ferryboat ride to Mukilteo, just south of Everett.

Driving is the fastest, but not the most intimate, way to experience this area. There are stimulating hikes to consider. Contact the **NATIONAL PARK SERVICE** at 800 State Street, Sedro Woolley, Washington 98284, and have them send you detailed maps of the area.

There is a network of graveled dirt roads off the main highways that lead to the paths less taken. These are treks of the heart for pleasure and adventure.

◆ **Romantic Prelude:** If you are heading out to the Cascades from Seattle on Interstate 90 and you want a remarkable overview of the scenery you'll be traveling through, consider stopping at **SNOQUALMIE WINERY**, 1000 Winery Road, Snoqualmie, (206) 888-4000 (watch for the signs next to the Snoqualmie Falls exit). The view of the mountains from the tasting room is unbelievable.

◆ **Romantic Ending:** On Highway 20, as you finish the last stretch of the Cascade Loop journey (or the beginning, depending on which direction you started from), the **DIABLO DAM OVERPASS** and **ROSS LAKE** will take your breath away. The vistas along this stretch of road are awesome.

NORTHERN WILDERNESS RIVER RIDERS

23312 77th Avenue, Woodinville
(206) 448-RAFT
Expensive

If you are interested in traveling any of the rivers in the region, call for information and directions on where to rendezvous with your guide.

The Skykomish, Klickitat, Methow, White Salmon, Toutle and Chiwawa rivers are sites for some of the most incredible rafting trips you can find. They are all visually exciting and relentlessly tumultuous. There are several river-rafting companies in the Northwest that provide professional guides to take you down these rivers. Northern Wilderness is a good, safe company that will provide you with solid information as well as one of their clever brochures.

Once you've made the decision about which river you want to negotiate, the rest is, if you will, all downstream. As you follow the tendril-like course the water has etched through the land, each coiling turn exposes a sudden change in perspective on the landscape. One turn may reveal grassy woods adjoining the quiet flow of peaceful water; another magically manifests a rocky, snowcapped tableau penetrated by a bursting mass of energy called white water. The raft's roller-coaster motion accentuates the thrill and glory of the landscape. And the sensation of cold water against your skin as you wildly paddle over and through a whirlpool can make your heart pound and your senses spin.

HAUS LORELEI BED & BREAKFAST, Leavenworth

347 Division Street
(509) 548-5726
Very Reasonable

From Highway 2, as you enter the town of Leavenworth from the west, turn south onto Ninth Street. Go two blocks and turn west onto Commercial and then south again onto Division. Division dead-ends at Haus Lorelei.

At Haus Lorelei the best of both worlds is available. You can be at the edge of Leavenworth's town center, yet have no evidence of that lively world only moments away. From the moment you enter this European country mansion you'll sense that relaxation is at hand and the stress of the world is somewhere else. This bed & breakfast offers an easygoing, informal winter or summer sojourn.

The dining and living room areas are partitioned by a massive, beach-stone fireplace. There is a huge screened porch that overlooks the expansive lawn and the Wenatchee River below. The sound of rushing whitewater can soothe the most stressed city nerves. The two downstairs bedrooms are huge and comfortable and decorated with magnificent antiques imported from Germany. Both of these rooms have private baths. (The two rooms upstair — one is dormitory-style — share a bath and are designed more for groups or families.) In the morning, as you take time over a breakfast of crepes and fresh fruit, your easygoing hostess can help you plan a rewarding day.

◆ *Romantic Warning:* There are a number of people — and I'm one of them — who do not think the town of Leavenworth is romantic. My misgivings are due to the town's blatantly repetitive Bavarian theme and tourist attractions. The Germanic ski-lodge influence is robust in a beerfest, crowds-galore sort of way, and it doesn't leave much room for tender snuggling or quiet moments. And this town can get crowded. Still, Leavenworth has something for everyone and you'll find some romantic alternatives that enable the softer side of the town to be yours — like cross-country skiing, hiking, white-water rafting, daydreaming, quiet restaurants, picnics and more.

MOUNTAIN HOME LODGE, Leavenworth
P.O. Box 687
(509) 548-7077
Moderate

Head north from Seattle on Interstate 5. Just south of Everett, take Highway 2 to Leavenworth. East of town, immediately past the bridge over the Wenatchee River, turn right on Duncan Road. Duncan Road will connect with Mountain Home Road which will take you directly to the lodge. In winter the prearranged pickup area is just west of Duncan Road; call for specific directions to the rendezvous point.

If seclusion is something you dream about, and being taken care of is what you crave, you can come to Mountain Home Lodge and find the perfect balance of the two. The substantial wood lodge is cradled atop a private mountain meadow, and the staff here will graciously tend to all your needs. The only way to reach the lodge during the winter is via prearranged snowcat pickup. Your rendezvous point will be just outside Leavenworth on Highway 2, from which it is a half-hour trip up the mountainside to the isolated accommodations of the lodge. The slow journey up will offer views of the quiet river valley twinkling with lights from the village shops and streets of Leavenworth. Be prepared for a quiet ascent punctuated only by the sounds of crunching snow and your "oohs" and "aahs" of amazement.

When you arrive during winter, the mountain and meadow will be completely covered by snow. The steam from the hot tub will drift lazily into the air and disappear. Your room will be unassuming though very comfortable, with a view of the snow-covered landscape. The fireplace in the shared living area is next to the small dining room where you will be served three mountain-fresh, country-style meals every day. Wall-to-wall windows allow you to watch the winter weather in its full white glory as you soak up the warmth and hospitality of the interior. Cross-country skiing, snowmobiling and sledding are all at your doorstep. During the summer months Mountain Home Lodge is easily accessible and can still be just as private and exciting. Without the snow's enchanting limitations, horseback riding, restaurants and hiking are nearby.

◆ **Romantic Note:** During the winter there is no safe way to drive here, so the restaurant is for guests only and meals are included in the price of accommodations. But during the summer anyone can make reservations for meals here, even if you don't stay overnight.

PENSION ANNA, Leavenworth
926 Commercial Street
(509) 548-6273
Inexpensive to Expensive

From Highway 2 in the town of Leavenworth, turn left on 9th Street to Commercial and turn left again. The pension is on the corner of 9th and Commercial.

The Austrian farmhouse design of this brand-new bed & breakfast seems almost cliched in a town where every other storefront manifests the same theme. Though it looks nice enough from the outside, one can only take so much theme-living at a time. Once inside, though, all the triteness dissolves and you are escorted to a beautiful, stately room complete with white, thick down comforters, down pillows, lush carpeting, stately armoire, tiled private bath and plenty of space and comfort (and, in the summer, air conditioning). This is one of the few places where the inexpensive rooms are just as wonderful as the higher priced ones. That's not to say that the King and Queen Suites aren't more luxurious and spacious — complete with spa tubs, fireplaces and sitting areas with cushy sofas. But even without spas and fireplaces, the other rooms are every bit as desirable. A continental breakfast is served in a congenial room on the main floor where tables for two and carved wood chairs are placed around a wood banquette.

RUN OF THE RIVER BED & BREAKFAST,
Leavenworth

9308 East Leavenworth Road
(509) 548-7171
Moderate

Call for reservations and directions.

Run of the River wrote and asked me to come and take a look. They said that their place was a "hidden jewel" and would be a good kissing addition to my book. As usual, I was immediately skeptical. All bed & breakfast owners think their place is romantic, and believe me, it's not often true. Plus everything in the brochure they sent me sounded too good to be true: a natural log-cabin contemporary home with cathedral ceilings of pine, picture windows overlooking a spectacular view of the Cascades, the winding Icicle River a stone's throw from each room, luxurious suites with handcrafted log beds, antique quilts, personal terrycloth robes and access to a large wraparound deck and patio. Two of the rooms downstairs, designed for couples traveling together, have woodstoves, and the Rose Suite upstairs has a private spa tub, plus there is a huge hot tub set near the river in a log pavilion at the back of the house.

Yes, too good to be true, until you arrive and learn that their description is an understatement. The entire place is supreme: the country-cozy rooms, the lush down comforters, firm beds, floor-to-ceiling windows throughout and the loft reading areas in each of the suites — all are perfect. Even breakfast served around one large table in the dining room is a hearty, lavish affair worthy of an award.

It won't take long before it becomes difficult to get a room here; this hidden jewel won't stay hidden. How could anyone possibly not want to come back?

THE TERRACE BISTRO, Leavenworth
200 Eighth Street
(509) 548-4193
Inexpensive to Moderate

Just off 8th Street, in the alley between Commercial and Front Streets.

The Terrace Bistro is considered by almost all the townspeople I talked with to be the best restaurant for miles around. The handsome, cozy upstairs location and rooftop dining area are the venues for a baronial-style dining experience. High wood-backed chairs with scarlet cushions, floral carpeting, and white stucco walls with soft lighting create a rich atmosphere. For an intimate meal in and around Leavenworth, this is one of the premier spots, and the food is excellent.

◆ *Romantic Alternative:* BISTRO HOFBRAU, 820 Commercial, (509) 548-6125, (Moderate) is owned and operated by the same people who own The Terrace Bistro, and the result is equally good: excellent cuisine and handsome, intimate surroundings, just as at The Terrace, only here (despite the German name) there's a decidedly Italian flare. The menu is small but the entrees were first-rate, and the cannelloni in particular was wonderful. Both restaurants are set far enough away from the main street of Leavenworth to give relief from the tourist crowds.

ICICLE OUTFITTERS & GUIDES, Leavenworth
P.O. Box 322
(509) 784-1145
Moderate

Call for their brochure, reservations and directions to their location on the south shore of Lake Wenatchee.

A great way to encounter this land is to take a trek on horseback, and Icicle Outfitters & Guides is a unique Cascades company that provides everything from hourly rides to an overnight pack trip. Overnight journeys come complete with meals, pack horses, saddle horses, a well-seasoned wrangler, cook, tents and the entire camp setup for a 2-to-7-day expedition. This is one unbelievable adventure. You'll cross unspoiled wilderness where pure mountain lakes and streams glisten in the sunshine, the wind rushes through the trees, hawks soar overhead and the snow-capped mountains tower above. As you warm yourself around the roaring campfire at night, after the hearty, freshly cooked dinner is served and cleared, you will find yourselves at peace with each other and the world.

SILVER BAY INN, Stehekin
Box 43
(509) 682-2212
Inexpensive

Take Highway 2 heading east past Leavenworth, toward Wenatchee. Follow the signs for Highway 97 North. This will take you to the town of Chelan, where you can catch the boat to Stehekin. For information on scheduled departures call (509) 682-2022 or (800)-4CHELAN. Hikers will want to check with the National Park Service for the backpacking route to Stehekin.

The town of Stehekin is geographically unique. It is accessible only by ferryboat (no cars) from Chelan, or a hike over the mountains via high-country trails. Lake Chelan is renowned for its glorious, dramatic scenery. The towering mountains that line this 55-mile lake are breathtaking against the cool blue of the glacier-fed waters. The exquisite ferry crossing takes approximately 4 hours and there is only one round-trip crossing a day. Stehekin tends to be a bit crowded with ferry passengers in the afternoon, but because most of them stay only for the day, once the boat leaves, in the late afternoon, only the romantics remain and the town is serenely peaceful once more.

Silver Bay Inn, the local bed & breakfast, is a special place to stay — not just because of its solar window construction or cozy, windowed breakfast nook. And not just because of the wondrous views from its deck and rooms, or the tempting espresso breakfasts. It's special because of the extreme isolation of the location, which makes this spot a Northwest must for those who want to get away from it all.

SUN MOUNTAIN LODGE, Winthrop
P.O. Box 1000
(509) 996-2211
Inexpensive to Expensive

Follow Highway 97 north toward Pateros. At Pateros turn northwest onto Highway 153 and follow the Methow River toward Twisp. Take Highway 20 through Twisp on to Winthrop. From there follow the signs to the lodge.

If I had several million dollars to spend on a renovation, I would want it to end up looking like this. Every aspect of the recently remodeled Sun Mountain Lodge is remarkable and stunning. The drive alone is well worth the trip. The winding road up to this mountaintop resort allows for a sweeping view of the rugged, sculpted peaks and the golden Methow River Valley below. The new main building and lobby area are made out of massive timbers and stone, and the interior is graced by immense wrought-iron chandeliers, stone flooring and rock-clad fire-places. All of the rooms in the main lodge are beautifully appointed, though a bit hotel-like, and most have panoramic viewing windows (some overlook the roof). The suites, in a separate wing across from the lodge, are impeccable places to stay. Each unit has its own fireplace, stone patio, glass sliding doors, willow furnishings, lush comforters and the ability to cross-country ski out your back door. And the views from here are mesmerizing. Other stellar amenities include two heated pools, hiking trails, horseback riding, exercise equipment, mountain bikes and the most effortless tranquility imaginable.

If you've decided not to take advantage of the premium accommodations, at least take the time to stop for a while at the restaurant housed in the original section of the lodge. The developers were wise enough to leave well enough alone, because this part of the lodge was and is flawless. From every position you can allow your eyes to feast on the surroundings that are food for the soul. The deck wraps around the outside and brings you face to face with the grandeur of the area. Surprisingly enough, the menu is impressive, the service excellent and the entrees and desserts delicious. The kitchen is particularly well-known for its applewood-smoked duck. Hold hands tightly; this place, from kiss to kiss, is truly amazing.

◆ *Romantic Note:* Sun Mountain Lodge offers totally outrageous, thoroughly intoxicating helicopter-skiing packages for both downhill and cross-country skiers. There are virgin powder runs that will leave you breathless for months to come. At the end of the day, you will need to cuddle very close and review your feats of athletic prowess.

THE MAZAMA COUNTRY INN, Mazama

P.O. Box 223
(509) 996-2681
Inexpensive

Fourteen miles north of Winthrop on Highway 20, watch for the signs to the inn.

The Mazama Inn is in the middle of nowhere, and that is one of its most attractive points. Set in the heart of the forest at the foot of a mountainside, the inn has a handful of units that are simple, clean and unassuming, which would be a romantic drawback if it weren't for their sensational views and the amenities available both winter and summer. Everything is here for you — horseback riding, helicopter skiing, cross-country skiing, mountain bicycling, wind surfing, sleigh riding, a sauna, a hot tub placed in a garden setting, and a country-style restaurant that serves three wonderful meals a day. The breakfasts are generous and the dinner offerings are a creative, seasonal selection of meats, fresh fish and pasta. The interior is soothing and calming. Gently swaying boughs grace the tall windows, and the floor-to-ceiling stone fireplace keeps the room toasty warm. The Mazama Country Inn is an easy, casual setting for playing and sharing treasured moments.

Note: During the winter, the meals are included in one reasonably priced, excellent package.

MOUNT RAINIER

For area information call (206) 569-2211. Many roads lead to Mount Rainier National Park: from Enumclaw on the north and Yakima on the east, take Highway 410 into the park. Highway 12 from both the southeast and southwest intersects with Highway 123, which will take you into the park. On the southwest side of the park, Highway 7 intersects with Highway 706 at the town of Elbe. Highway 706 goes right into the park and takes you straight to Paradise, literally and figuratively.

Poetic words to describe Mount Rainier are better left to the laureates. For the kissing purposes of this book, suffice it to say that almost every inch of this mountain is quintessentially romantic and outrageously exquisite. From its dormant volcanic heart to its eternally glacier-covered peaks, Mount Rainier is guaranteed to provide superlative panoramic views, memorable hikes and crystal clear memories. If it's Northwest drama and passion you yearn for, this volcano has it.

◆ **Romantic Note:** Mount Rainier is only one of several dormant volcanoes around these parts. Less traveled than Mount Rainier are Mount Baker, just south of the Canadian border, and Mount Adams, just north of the Oregon border. All three of these mountains hold out good prospects for unrestrained messing around.

◆ **Second Romantic Note:** Several park roads, including some of the main routes onto the mountain, are closed during the winter, so always check for seasonal accessibility. There are excellent hiking books available for this region from Mountaineers Books. For their catalog, write to 306 Second Avenue W., Seattle, 98119, (206) 285-2665.

CHINOOK PASS, Mount Rainier

If you're in the Mount Baker-Snoqualmie National Forest on the east side of Mount Rainier, Highway 410 will take you through the pass.

On a fall afternoon, Chinook Pass becomes almost too glorious. You'll be so excited about the scenery, you might finish touring and forget to kiss. Take a moment to conjure up the image of golden light bathing hills and lakes. Notice the vivid leaf-shades of red and amber that brocade the trees and meadows. Feel the fall air brush your skin at the same time solar heat tempers that chill. Sigh . . . This is a visual gift to share with each other.

◆ *Romantic Note:* The drive through the pass is loaded with vista turnoffs, hikes with dizzying switchbacks, and meadows which you can explore side by side. The only caution is to travel prepared. Comfortable hiking shoes, munchies (lots of munchies), water bottle, tissues and a day-pack will make Chinook Pass a more passable experience. Also be considerate of the wilderness. Trails are for people, the rest of the area is for the animals and plants. This considerate behavior on the part of all visitors will keep the beauty intact for many more years to come.

SUNRISE, Mount Rainier

From the north or east, take Highway 410 into Mount Rainier National Park and follow the park map to Sunrise.

If you've always wondered what it must be like at the top of the world, come to Sunrise and fulfill your fantasy, for this is in fact as close to the top of the world as you can drive in the continental United States. When you arrive, there are so many inspiring trails (some relatively easy) to pick from that choosing might be harder than you'd like. Your day hike can be a level, leisurely stroll or a strenuous trek up a mountain path, far away from everyone and everything except each other. You will never hear such silence.

EMERALD RIDGE, Mount Rainier

This area of Mount Rainier is on the west face of the mountain near the Highway 706 entrance to the park. One mile after you enter the park there will be a left turn that takes you on an unpaved road along Emerald Ridge. This road is open only during the summer and, due to washout, has occasionally been closed then as well. Be sure to call the ranger station for the status of this area.

The entire west side of Mount Rainier is a challenge made for daring companions who own a four-wheel-drive Jeep or truck. The road is a remnant of a logging path, so it is not often driven on. The trails off this road are hiked even less. Finding your own special spot will be hard on your car and you, but worth every bounce of the steep ascent.

MIO AMORE PENSIONE, Trout Lake
P.O. Box 208
(509) 395-2264
Moderate

From Highway 14 on the north side of the Columbia River Gorge, near White Salmon, head north on Highway 141 to Trout Lake. As you enter the town, watch for the signs to Mio Amore.

For some reason, Mount Adams isn't lauded as much as the other sights in the Cascades. Yet this inactive volcano is in a unique position at the south end of Washington state, juxtaposed between the green, lush forests of the western half and the rain shadow of the eastern half. The wine country in these parts adds a majestic distinction, surrounding the base of the mountain with rolling manicured vineyards. And the endless recreational activities here provide all the outdoor entertainment requisite for a Northwest escape.

Mio Amore Pensione rests at the foot of Mount Adams, whose snowcapped peaks and rolling hills tower over its backyard. This Victorian home has been renovated into a wonderful bed & breakfast with rustic rooms and tender touches all about. There is even a suite with a sitting area and private bath. Yet the highlight of your stay will be the gourmet morning meal and four-course evening meal served by the innkeepers every day.

Breakfast is complimentary for those staying at the Pensione. This eye-opening meal is graciously served and consists of luscious home-made tortes, breads and specialty Italian baked dishes. Dinner is an array of exotic meats and fresh fish, selected on a daily basis by the first couple to book their reservation. Mio Amore is one of the few places where you can combine a mountain exploration with gourmet feasting, and it's a relaxing place in which to pamper yourselves in proverbial Northwest style and seclusion.

◆ *Romantic Note:* Reservations for dinner are accepted even if you are not staying overnight. Also be aware that the home is small and if you are not participating in dinner, you will hear the experience from the upstairs rooms between 7 P.M. and 9:30 P.M. anyway.

◆ *A Romantic Must:* On your way to or from Mount Adams, be certain to stop at **CHARLES HOOPER FAMILY WINERY,** Spring Creek Road, Husum 98623, (509) 493-2324. (Call first to check seasonal hours.) A picnic or stroll through the vineyards treats you to one of the most exquisite views you'll behold anywhere. Take the time for this one; your eyes, palates and hearts will be forever grateful.

INN OF THE WHITE SALMON, White Salmon

172 Jewett
(509) 493-2335
Moderate

From Highway 14, follow Highway 141 a short distance to the town of White Salmon. The inn is at the north end of town on the right-hand side of the road.

For romantic purposes, a bed & breakfast needs to be more than just a place that serves a good breakfast. I have never recommended a place simply for that one feature — until now, that is. The Inn of the White Salmon is located on a fairly commercial street (commercial for these parts) in a less than attractive part of town. The rooms are old, dim and musty, with no views and no redeeming features. But all of that melts into oblivion when you wake up to the breakfast feast served faithfully every morning in the inn's quaint dining room.

> *"A love song is just a caress set to music."*
> **Sigmund Romberg**

PORTLAND AREA

Once you visit Portland, you are likely to become an enthusiast. This growing municipality has two distinct personalities — one is urban and the other rural. There is an impressive amount of greenery here, and an amazing variety of terrain for walking, hiking and dawdling. Gardens, parks, forest and islands blanket the landscape, and are all beautiful and meticulously maintained. Then there's the urban part of Portland's character: the upscale charm of Nob Hill, a renovated neighborhood overflowing with restaurants and shops; the growing downtown center dotted with art deco buildings and glass skyscrapers shaping the skyline; a restored old-town area with all its vintage charm left intact; and the recently developed, affluent riverfront area called Riverplace. And both these personalities are in perfect balance. This is what makes Portland so remarkable — city life is only tolerated if it doesn't get in the way of the countryside. Whether you are visiting for a day or a week, this city's earthy appeal is bound to make a loving impression.

◆ Hotel/Bed & Breakfast Kissing ◆

THE HERON HAUS, Portland
2545 N.W. Westover Road
(503) 274-1846
Moderate to Very Expensive

Please call for reservations and directions.

The bed & breakfast style of lodging is known for being cozy, warm and congenial. Nothing is quite so affection-producing as a stay in a home where the owners diligently tend to their guests' hearts and senses. That includes the wafting aroma of just-baked morning pastries, a roaring fireplace, cushy furnishings, snuggly quilts covering over-size pillows, and a conspicuous amount of tender loving care. The Heron Haus has all this and more.

The home is a huge (7,500 square feet), attractively furnished mansion almost entirely given over to the guests. There is also a sundeck, pool, and four spacious sun-filled suites with cozy sitting areas. The bathrooms are so spectacular that you may decide to stay in them and forget about returning to your bed. One suite has an ample spa tub that overlooks the city, and another has a shower with seven nozzles which cover every inch of you with pulsating water. With space to spare, Heron Haus can accommodate couples who want to emerge clean, giggling and inseparable.

THE HEATHMAN HOTEL, Portland
Broadway at Salmon Street
(503) 241-4100
Moderate

Look for clearly marked signs on Highway 405 for Market Street or City Center. Market and Broadway intersect; turn north onto Broadway. Salmon Street is a few blocks north.

When you walk into the lobby of The Heathman, your first reaction will be one of Northwest skepticism. While the geometric art and marble detailing that fills the interior may look distinguished and striking, the modern design and hard finishes make a cold, stark impression. Perhaps the coziest part of the hotel is the Tea Court. The classic decor, solid teak paneling, large fireplace and genial quiet make this a suitable place for an afternoon of thoughtful conversation and warm gazes.

The restaurant at The Heathman Hotel is considered to be one of the finest around. Attentive service and skillfully prepared dishes make for a memorable evening of fine dining. Breakfast is an elegant affair, as carefully created as dinner. The only drawback here is the business conversations taking place around you. But after dinner, when you retire to your elegant (though small) room, there will no longer be a need for suits, ties, heels or briefcases, and then you can really let your hair down.

◆ *Romantic Alternative:* **THE BENSON**, 309 S.W. Broadway, (503) 228-2000 (Expensive) is a grand old hotel with one of the most massive, ornate lobbies you will see anywhere in the Northwest. The chandeliered, wood-paneled interior is stunning and the seating intimate and quiet. Up until now, that was pretty much all that was remarkable at The Benson, but a $16 million renovation, scheduled for completion in January 1991, is presumed to be changing all of that. The rooms will be much larger and the interiors are to be elegantly designed. If it can get away from hotel-basic, The Benson could be quite the place to stay in downtown Portland.

MACMASTER HOUSE BED & BREAKFAST, Portland

1041 S.W. Vista Avenue
(503) 223-7362
Inexpensive to Moderate

Call for reservations and directions.

There are many things about this turn-of-the-century mansion that are impressive and reminiscent of grand old-world living. There are also some things that could stand a bit of sprucing up. As you walk up to the house, the formal portico with Doric columns and Palladian windows of leaded glass is a bit run-down and in need of paint and landscaping. Once inside, however, there is a bright, airy feeling all around, though some new rugs and paint could help in here too. The suites are all handsome and lush, four have fireplaces, most have separate sitting areas, and The MacMaster Suite has a deck with a view. Large windows, comfortable beds and attractive furnishings are all well maintained and attractive. The rooms with private baths are definitely the best.

MUMFORD MANOR
1130 S.W. King
(503) 243-2443
Moderate

Call for reservations and directions.

From the moment you enter this brilliantly renovated Victorian house in the affluent neighborhood of King's Hill, you will be eager to stay. The formal hall is flanked on either side by two sumptuous sitting rooms that are warmed by huge antique fireplaces and fronted by French doors that open to the garden patio. Upstairs the four guestrooms — each with its own private bath, sitting room, and large windows — are beautifully decorated with country floral fabrics. Every corner of this bed & breakfast is exceedingly comfortable and wonderfully romantic. Even the breakfast is delectable. When you awake, the aromas of such delicacies as filbert waffles, chocolate croissants and fresh-squeezed orange juice may greet you in the sun-filled dining room.

◆ *Romantic Alternative:* **PORTLAND'S WHITE HOUSE**, 1914 N.E. 22nd Avenue, (503) 287-7131 (Inexpensive to Moderate) has Greek columns, a fountain, a circular driveway and a white exterior with a west wing and an east wing. This impressive structure does indeed resemble its Washington, D.C. namesake. Inside the similarities stop, but the bed & breakfast refinement continues. The real reason to come here is not so much for the bed & breakfast rooms on the second floor, even though they are nice enough and scrupulously maintained. Come instead for your wedding, so that the reception can happen on the lower levels and the bridal party can take over the rooms upstairs. The owner of the White House is a catering specialist and turns her house over for special parties three times a month. If you want to stay just for the bed & breakfast, the accommodations are gracious and the morning breakfast is wonderful. Weekends can prove a bit hectic when an event is taking place, but during the week everything is sedate and composed.

◆ Restaurant Kissing ◆

ATWATER'S RESTAURANT, Portland
111 S.W. Fifth Avenue
(503) 220-3629
Very Expensive

On Fifth and Burnside in downtown Portland, at the top of the U.S. Bancorp Tower. From Highway 405, follow the City Center exit to Fourth Avenue. Turn north on Fourth Avenue and west on Pine Street. This will take you to a parking garage under the building.

Atwater's Restaurant, atop Portland's tallest building, proclaims that it is designed to look like an exclusive uptown residence. From the Oriental-style elevator doors to the silver service, marble floors and other extravagant finishing touches, it is clear that this is an ultra-formal dining establishment. The service is attentive, almost to the point of hovering, but the food is superior (they serve a lavish Sunday brunch) and artistically served. From this vantage point on cloud nine you can watch the downtown buildings reflect the sun's light until only a silhouette of mountains is visible through the floor-to-ceiling windows.

CAFÉ DES AMIS, Portland

1987 N.W. Kearney Street
(503) 295-6487
Moderate to Expensive

Take N.W. Lovejoy west to 19th Avenue and turn south for one block to
Kearney Street. The café is at the intersection of Kearney and 19th.

Café des Amis effectively blends a Northwest atmosphere with
epicurean French cuisine and is considered one of the best dining spots
in Portland. The food is a gastronomic treat. The room is simply adorned
with wood tables well-spaced from each other, white walls and white
starched-linen tablecloths. There's a cordiality about the place that
makes for a totally romantic culinary experience. The patés are delicious,
the duck, quail and salmon are perfectly prepared, and the New York
steak is the thickest and tenderest you may ever taste. The delectable
dessert is a masterstroke.

PAISLEY'S, Portland

1204 N.W. 21st Avenue
(503) 243-2403
Moderate

From downtown Portland, go west on N.W. Lovejoy Street to 21st Avenue
and turn left. Paisley's is at the intersection of Northrup Street and 21st.

Paisley's is located in the heart of Portland's Nob Hill, which is blessed
with over 40 lovingly renovated neighborhood shops and restaurants,
each one more interesting than the next and several among the best
Portland has to offer. Paisley's lives up to this area's reputation with its
dedication to fine cooking in a relaxed setting. The attention the new
owner has given to maintaining an attractive, unpretentious place is
reflected in the modest interior filled with wood tables, finished wood
floors, pastel artwork and soft lighting. There is also outdoor seating on
the front porch. Breakfast, lunch and dinner are all well done and

graciously served. Save room for the desserts here, which are as delicious to hear described as they are to eat. The aroma of robust cappuccino and delicate souffles, tortes, tarts and brulees will sweep you off your feet.

GENOA'S
2832 S.E. Belmont Street
(503) 238-1464
Expensive

On Belmont between 28th and 29th Avenues.

If discreet dining is what you're looking for in Portland, come to this small storefront location in the southeast section of the city. You can't see inside; cranberry-colored window coverings keep outsiders out and insiders from seeing anything of the outside world — including light. Your focus will be strictly directed on the food and each other. Once you adapt to the sultry lighting, you'll find a five-course parade of Italian delicacies that will keep your attention throughout the entire evening.

LA MIRABELLE, Portland
1126 S.W. 18th Avenue
(503) 223-7113
Expensive

On 18th between Main and Jefferson Streets. The restaurant is open for dinner only, Thursday through Saturday.

The run-down exterior of this old building gives no indication of the gracious world that lies inside on the ground level. Lace-covered windows seem incongruous from the outside, but once inside you'll find a luxurious Renaissance-style atmosphere and exquisite French food. Banquettes in floral upholstery line the wall, and white starched linen tablecloths set with fine china and crystal sparkle against the white-washed walls. There are three small dining salons at La Mirabelle, and though the service can be a bit pompous it is efficient. The entire experience is exceptional.

WESTERN CULINARY INSTITUTE, Portland
1316 S.W. 13th Avenue
(503) 223-2245
Inexpensive

Call for reservations and directions.

I do not exaggerate when I say that there isn't a kitchen staff anywhere in the Northwest that tries harder than the folks here. This is the only cooking school of its kind in the region, and the enthusiastic talent that is drawn here is impressive. There are over 25 enthusiastic, accommodating culinary students who create elaborate dishes for an ever-changing menu.

The restaurant is open Monday through Friday for both lunch and dinner. "Simple but elegant" is the key phrase here, along with the consoling word "inexpensive." The food is not always excellent, but it is consistently intriguing and usually good. Besides, at these prices almost anybody can afford to be a romantic gourmet.

◆ Outdoor Kissing ◆

MACLEAY PARK, Portland

Macleay Park is one of many entrances to Portland's Forest Park. You can enter Macleay off the Thurman Bridge near Franklin and 32nd Street N.W., or at the end of Forest Park in northwest Portland off Cornell Road.

Macleay Park is a park within a park and a gorgeous example of nature's ability to thrive in the midst of a city. This is a lush green wilderness strewn with surging creeks and hiking trails. It is just one of the almost limitless doorways into Portland's immense backyard called Forest Park, which is regarded as the largest city-wilderness in the United States. It affords so many kissing places that if you're not careful, you'll risk a lip or two.

◆ *Romantic Note:* COLLINS' SANCTUARY, run by the Portland Audubon Society, 5151 N.W. Cornell Road, (503) 292-6855, is another doorway into Forest Park, and not very well known even though its secluded beauty is near the heart of the city. There are trails and paths that will lead you to private corners of this 67-acre wildlife area.

RIVERPLACE, Portland

1510 S.W. Harbor Way. From downtown Portland take S.W. Market Street east to the river, where it will dead-end at Riverplace.

Personally, I don't find Riverplace the least bit romantic. How can a half-mile-long arcade of condominiums, stores and restaurants be intimate and endearing? But when I visited this Willamette River development I saw so many couples strolling hand-in-hand that I decided to include Riverplace anyway. I'll try to give you a romantic perspective on this place, out of a sense of fairness.

Riverplace begins with the European refinement and poshness of the **ALEXIS HOTEL** at the northern tip of the walk. Here you have an exquisite European-style building with high quality, hotel-like accommodations and a distinctive, much-admired restaurant. The lobby bar here is one of the most romantic in town. As you continue walking you'll have the water on one side and a series of handsome condominiums on the other. There are a dozen or so boutiques and eateries here. Further down are more restaurants with water views.

Admittedly, this is a lovely development and there are enough options here to offer something for everyone regardless of taste or budget. Romantic or not, Riverplace is worth a stroll and perhaps a stop somewhere along the way for a glass of wine or a shot of espresso, a quick disco beat, or whatever else may be alive and happening.

SAUVIE ISLAND

Go north on Highway 30 to the Sauvie Island Bridge, about 11 miles from downtown Portland. There is a small day-use fee for a visit to the island.

When you feel the need for wide-open empty space, take a drive to this vast pastoral oasis. Sauvie Island is a popular Portland getaway, but its size prevents it from ever feeling crowded. There are relatively isolated beaches and numerous hiking trails through wetlands, pasture, oak woodlands and spotty sections of coniferous forest. Oak Island is a much smaller land mass, attached by a natural bridge at the northeast end of Sauvie Island, where stretches of sandy beach are available.

◆ *Romantic Warning:* Sauvie Island can be covered in smog when other parts of the area are clear. Check the horizon before setting out for the island. No drinking water or gasoline is available here.

SKYLINE DRIVE, Portland

Portland's Forest Park is a vast wilderness on the west side of the Willamette River. At the park's south end, Cornell Road intersects with Skyline Drive. Skyline Drive borders the east side of the park.

Is it possible for city roads or highways to spiral up and around to celestial splendor? If so, Skyline Drive is a likely candidate and a quick or slow cruise over this winding road will help you cast a deciding vote. There are three miles of fascinating vistas that outline the eastern boundary of Forest Park. At the crest you can view the contours of the Cascades, the Willamette Valley awash in colors of green, the gentle forms of the coastal mountain range, and the skyline of downtown Portland. If you want to get up and away without having to go far from the city, cruise Skyline Drive any time of day or night.

◆ *Romantic Suggestion:* There is a school located at 11536 N.W. Skyline Drive, which is smack-dab atop this marvelous scenic road. When school isn't in session, I suggest that you two play on the swing or the slide, both of which are excellent pieces of equipment for courtship. The sunsets here are also worth a brief romp in the schoolyard.

TRYON CREEK STATE PARK, Portland

Head south from Portland on Interstate 5 to the Terwilliger exit. Travel 2½ miles due south on S.W. Terwilliger Boulevard to get to the park.

This is the place for easy walks along gently rolling red-bark paths through thick forestland. Don't expect wide vistas or places to sit in the sun. It is almost always shady and moist here, not to mention a little muddy in the winter. But whether you walk for miles or just a few hundred feet, the two of you will feel safe, unhurried and alone here.

WASHINGTON PARK ROSE GARDENS, Portland

From downtown Portland, drive west on W. Burnside, following the signs to the gardens.

Washington Park Rose Gardens is a perfect lovers-lane hideout. The road to the tree-shaded parking area winds up a long, steep hill to a summit where the park itself reigns supreme over the city and the Willamette Valley. From the fragrant, endless rows of rosebushes to the exotic Japanese Gardens and the unhindered view of Portland and the mountains beyond, this is pure embracing territory, acre after magnificent acre. It's a perfect place to come for quiet afternoons, brilliant sunsets or twinkling evening lights.

WINE COUNTRY

*For more detailed information about the various tours through this region, send for a copy of the booklet **Discover Oregon Wineries**, 1359 W. 5th Avenue, Eugene, 97402, (503) 233-2377.*

A 45-minute drive southwest from Portland will bring you into wine country: rolling hills, golden grass and rows of grapes twined around poles to help their growth toward the sun. There are a number of wineries scattered within this picturesque area, each with its own attitude about what makes for a good glass of wine. Whether or not you are wine connoisseurs, you'll enjoy the calm and harmony of the Yamhill and Washington County countryside.

The dozen or so wineries of the valley all boast a robust wine selection, a rathskeller tasting room and a reposeful country setting that adds to your palatal experience. Some of these cellars are antique-laden homes, others are crowned by tantalizing views and idyllic gardens, while still others are plain buildings with row after row of grapevines. Whether you choose to visit one or all, and whether you choose to imbibe or not, your entire winery-hopping jaunt will be an intoxicating joy.

If you are a veteran wine-taster, then you have Shangri-la at hand. As you gallivant from winery to winery sampling the various proud offerings of each vineyard, you'll have the opportunity to experience an all-day non-stop picnic. You only need to bring along the cheese, bread, smoked salmon, and fruit.

◆ *Romantic Suggestions:* **TUALATIN VINEYARDS,** on Seavey Road, Route 1, Box 339, Forest Grove 97116, (503) 357-5005, and **ELK COVE VINEYARDS**, on 27751 N.W. Olson Road, Gaston 97119, (503) 985-7760, are two exceptional wineries in Yamhill County. Tualatin has a picnic area shaded by cherry trees that overlooks the valley and vineyards. Elk Cove has breathtaking views from its attractive tasting room, and there are picnic tables set on a grassy knoll. Both have award-winning wines that will perfectly enhance this dream-like country outing.

◆ *Romantic Options:* You may wish to extend your tryst in the tasting rooms by staying at a nearby bed & breakfast. The best way to do that is to stay either at **OWL'S VIEW BED & BREAKFAST**, P.O. Box 732, Newberg 97132, (503) 538- 6498 (Inexpensive to Expensive), or **ORCHARD VIEW INN**, 16540 N.W. Orchard View Road, McMinnville 97128, (503) 472-0165 (Inexpensive). Owl's View sits on a hill overlooking the valley, and Orchard View is nestled in a country neighborhood and has deer prancing around the backyard.

"Love is the answer, but while you are waiting for the answer, kissing raises some pretty good questions."

OREGON COAST

THE COAST

Follow Highway 101 south from Astoria at the Washington state border to Brookings at the California state border.

It is probably safe to say that no other state has a span of highway quite like Highway 101 in Oregon. This road hugs large sections of the coast and almost every one of those miles allows consistent visual contact with the scenery. The drive is literally breathtaking. Thank goodness there are many turnoffs, parks, hikes, undiscovered coves, rocky inlets and ravines where you can stop and drink in the view at your own leisurely pace.

The drama of this area is enhanced by the constant, temperamental mood-swings of the weather. At times the mixture of fog and sea mist creates a diffuse screen through which the world appears like an apparition. Other moments bring a disturbing quiet as a tempest brews in the distance where ocean and sky meet and bond as one. Yet even on the calmest of summer days, the unbridled energy and siren-song of the waves unleashing their power against beaches, headlands and haystack rocks has a spellbinding impact. The Oregon Coast is so beautiful that it can rekindle your relationship with each other and the world.

◆ *Romantic Note:* For information on Oregon Coast parks and recreation areas, call (503) 378-6305 or (503) 842-4981.

GILBERT INN, Seaside

341 Beach Drive
(503) 738-9770
Inexpensive

From Highway 101 head into the town of Seaside. When you reach the city center, turn south at Beach Drive and go two blocks to the inn.

There is absolutely nothing romantic about the town of Seaside. And when I say nothing, I *mean* nothing. This is a town where the ocean has been totally obscured by hyperactive developers with no sensitivity to the landscape. Arcades and boardwalks teem with kids. So why do I have a kissing entry in this unappealing location? Good question. But then you haven't seen Gilbert Inn.

Move this stunning bed & breakfast to almost any other setting in the Northwest and you would automatically have a four-lips place to spend exquisite time together. Everything about it is cozy and snug. All of the 10 rooms are delightfully renovated and have plenty of room and comfort. The new wing, added last year, is a series of brightly done rooms with private bathrooms that are decorated to blend creatively with each suite's fetching decor. Even the morning meal is notable and worthy of a stay in its own right.

So, the town of Seaside isn't romantic. But if you find yourself here, for whatever reason, be sure it's at Gilbert Inn.

CANNON BEACH

Cannon Beach is just west of Highway 101. Take Highway 26 from Portland west to Highway 101 and head south to Cannon Beach. Highway 30 from the north will also lead to Highway 101.

As you approach Cannon Beach it will be hard to believe your eyes — there is such an exhilarating procession of cliffs and ocean stretching to infinity. There are over seven miles of beach here, with firm sand and rolling waves that beckon dreamers and those in love to roll up their jeans and stroll along the shore hand-in-hand. The seascape is crowded with massive rock outcroppings, a key feature of this coastline. The hallmark of Cannon Beach is a freestanding monolith called Haystack Rock, the third largest of its kind in the world and a true natural wonder. At low tide you can stand at its threshold and feel humbled by its towering dimensions.

The nickname for the entire Oregon Coast is "Sunset Empire," and that's a most descriptive title. As the sun begins to settle into the ocean, brilliant colors radiate from the horizon, filling the sky like a golden aurora borealis. At first the light penetrates the clouds as a pale lavender-blue haze, transforming suddenly into an intense yellow-amber, culminating in a blazing red that seems to set the sky on fire. Then as dusk finalizes its entrance, the clouds fade to steel-blue-grey and the sky changes its countenance from cobalt blue to indigo. Slowly the moon takes a central place in the evening heavens, reflecting its presence on the surface of the water in platinum rays. When the weather cooperates, this performance occurs nightly at Cannon Beach and along the entire Oregon Coast.

◆ *Romantic Options:* **ECOLA STATE PARK** and **INDIAN BEACH** are just to the north of Cannon Beach off Highway 101. Usually state parks are not considered good places for conducting affectionate business. Though they may be well-kept and offer supreme scenery, they also tend to be crowded and inundated with RVs and kids. But the character of this area is so exceptional, the potency of the sights so remarkable, you'll not notice anyone but yourselves and the splendor of nature.

◆ *Romantic Warning:* On a warm summer day Cannon Beach is very crowded, with traffic and congestion that seem out of place in such a serene, tranquil setting. Consider the quiet towns of Manzanita or Oceanside (both described in this section) further south along the coast as an alternative to Cannon Beach on crowded summer weekends.

THE ARGONAUTA INN, Cannon Beach

188 Second Street
(503) 436-2601
Inexpensive to Expensive

In Cannon Beach, turn west off Highway 101 onto Sunset. Drive to Hemlock Street and turn south. At First Street turn west and then south again onto Larch Street. The Argonauta Inn is to the right of the dead-end.

For imaginative, rustic accommodations, The Argonauta Inn stands alone. The inn is a weathered seashore complex that houses three small, cozy apartments and a large oceanfront beach house set right at the center of everything Cannon Beach has to offer. The shore is at your front door and the town is at your back. Most of the details are too good to be true: glass-enclosed patios, fireplaces, complete kitchens, antiques, powerful panoramas. But then there are the drawbacks — like saggy beds, mildewy smells and tacky touches that are more secondhand than homey. All in all (mostly because of location), this is still one of the most interesting places to stay in Cannon Beach.

THE HEARTHSTONE INN, Tolovana Park
107 East Jackson
(503) 436-2266
Inexpensive

From Highway 101 turn off onto Beach Loop Road by-passing the center of Cannon Beach for Tolovana Park. The inn is at the intersection of Hemlock and Jackson streets.

For a coastal change of pace, particularly if the summer pace of the beach is a bit much for you and you want to be near the surf but not quite that near, The Hearthstone Inn is your answer. In an out-of-the-way corner of Tolovana Park, this unobtrusive, contemporary wood building, hidden by gently swaying willow trees, looks more like a residence than a lodging. Yet there are four generous studios inside, with vaulted cedar ceilings, beach-rock fireplaces, skylights, stained glass windows and fully equipped kitchens. The shore is a short walk away and accessible for an invigorating morning walk on compact, damp sand. All of this combines to create a refreshingly private and welcome place to stay.

◆ *Romantic Note:* On our last visit, it seems the wind was blowing in the wrong direction, which made the smoke from the fireplace fill the room instead of the chimney. Not great — but forgivable.

THE WAVES MOTEL, Cannon Beach

188 West Second Street
(503) 436-2205
Inexpensive to Moderate

In Cannon Beach, turn west off Highway 101 onto Sunset. Drive to Hemlock Street and turn south. At First Street turn west, then south again onto Larch Street. The Waves is to the right just before the dead-end.

This is as eclectic an assortment of beach accommodations as it gets. Located just behind The Argonauta Inn, The Waves Motel is a hodge-podge of accommodations; some have scintillating views of the ocean, most have kitchens, many have fireplaces, some sleep two, some sleep six. The interiors are mostly plain yet quite comfortable, except for a few ultra-rustic cottages that aren't recommended at all. Then there's the newer, modern wing with units that have neither fireplace, view or kitchen, but they're brand spanking new and extremely comfortable and attractive.

Now none of that sounds particularly endearing, but if you choose the units with the ocean views and fireplaces, particularly in the Flagship Buildings — now we're talking about cozy and warm. The resonant sounds of the surf against the steadfast shore is a welcome reminder of just how far you've left city life behind you.

THE WHITE HERON LODGE, Cannon Beach

346 North Spruce
(503) 436-2205
Moderate

Call for reservations and directions. Reservations are handled by The Waves Motel.

The White Heron Lodge is located on the beachfront just north of the main village of Cannon Beach. Even though the proximity to town is close, in this part of the world it is far enough to make a difference in the peacefulness of your surroundings. Seagrass grows nearby as the sand eventually gives way to a well-kept lawn. The modern construction consists of one Victorian-style fourplex with comfortably appointed, fully equipped apartments, and a contemporary duplex that is spacious enough for five. There are decks that look out to the shore, fireplaces that crackle with inviting warmth, a spa tub and lots of space to feel right at home while you spoil yourselves in utter relaxation and quiet.

SURFSAND RESORT, Cannon Beach

P.O. Box 219
(503) 436-2274
Moderate to Expensive

From Highway 101 follow the Cannon Beach Loop road to Hemlock Street and watch for the sign on the west side of the street.

How can it be possible that I am about to describe the romantic details of a Best Western motel? Such places are usually my model for describing what is *not* romantic about a particular location or accommodation. But the Surfsand Best Western is pretty darned good and rates both of those lips I have given it. Now let me explain why.

Our room was spacious, decorated in soft shades of mauve and gray. There was an outdoor deck with a perfect view of Haystack Rock (it also had a view of the parking lot, which wasn't perfect but still pretty good). A huge spa tub in the bedroom area provided a welcome, leisurely soak near the gas fireplace, which again wasn't perfect but it warmed the room quickly and there was no fuss or bother with wood and kindling. The bathroom was large and attractively done in white tiles and outfitted with colorful oversized towels. And in the adjoining building there was even a large indoor pool and enormous hot tub. Other, less glamorous, units in the older section of the property have a ringside ocean view of everything due west to the horizon. For location and quality, this place is definitely one to consider; just ignore the name.

◆ *Romantic Consideration:* **THE WAYFARER RESTAURANT,** 1190 Pacific Drive, (503) 436-1108 (Inexpensive to Moderate) is owned by Surfsand Resort and has one of the best view dining rooms in Cannon Beach. The interior is done in the same mauve and gray colors you'll find at the resort. The food is actually pretty good, though you'll do best to stick to the fresh-broiled selections or steamed clams and mussels.

TURK'S HOUSE, Cannon Beach
P.O. Box 482
(503) 436-1809
Expensive

Call for reservations and directions.

A few well written articles by travel writers, placed in some notable publications, have made Turk's House *the* place to stay in Cannon Beach. You have to forgive travel writers, though; after all, we are only doing our job, even though the results can mean that some choice places become so popular it's difficult to get reservations.

For starters you get the entire run of this 1,800-square-foot home settled on a forested hill with a compelling view of the Oregon coastline. The uniquely crafted building is supported by stilts on one side and built over the western slope of the hill on the other. The exterior is of rough-cut spruce and fir with a wraparound deck on the ocean side of the house. The interior is a stunning display of towering pine ceilings, floor-to-ceiling windows, a massive stone fireplace, a spacious, two-level master bedroom with a generous spa tub, open tile shower and exercise equipment. Breakfast is a private affair, stocked every morning in your own kitchen. From top to bottom you will be ecstatic with your stay here. You only have to book months in advance to assure yourselves your share of ecstasy.

CAFÉ DE LA MER, Cannon Beach
1287 South Hemlock Street
(503) 436-1179
Expensive

Just off the main street of Cannon Beach, near Dawes Street.

It doesn't get much better than this anywhere along the coast, both for romantic ambience or superlative cuisine. The small rustic interior has been elegantly put together, and the attentive staff consistently delivers enticing dinners, superior service and a generous amount of soothing atmosphere. The rose-colored, wood-paneled dining room, glass-enclosed patio and well-spaced seating area comprise the setting, and the kitchen's delectable presentations are the highlight. What a welcome change of pace from the casual ambience of almost every other dining spot along the coast.

OSWALD WEST STATE PARK

Ten miles south of Cannon Beach on the west side of Highway 101. Look for signs pointing the way.

Oswald West State Park is one of the most ideal, inspiring campgrounds in these parts — just ask any Northwest camping enthusiast. Its superior desirability has to do with its mode of access. In order to set up camp, you need to walk a quarter of a mile down a forest path, wheeling a cart they provide, with your things piled on top. This short jaunt tends to separate the serious campers from the featherweights and RVs. Besides giving you that much-needed privacy, you'll be in a forested setting within arm's reach of the water. There are footpaths that take you briskly down to the pounding surf. The scenery to the south is a succession of overlapping mountains jutting into the ocean, making a dark jagged profile against the distant skyline. The white sand, effervescent surf and rock-clad shore make exploring here a treasure hunt.

HUG POINT

A few miles south of Cannon Beach off Highway 101, watch for the signs to Hug Point.

If you find yourselves at Hug Point during low tide, give in to your childlike curiosities and permit those kids inside of yourselves to play for the duration of your stay here. The soaring cliffs along the beach at Hug Point are gouged with caves and crevasses of varying shapes and proportions. For the timid there are gentle tidepools and rocky fissures where you can easily observe marine life. For the more daring there are dark, ominous sea caves to hide in. When your exploring is done and the tide reclaims your playground, the grown-ups in you can finish out the day by watching the dazzling sunset over the Pacific.

THE INN AT MANZANITA, Manzanita
67 Laneda
(503) 368-6754
Moderate

Follow Highway 101 into the town of Manzanita. Laneda is the main road through this small town. The inn is located one block from the ocean.

This petite village bordering the ocean is a relatively undiscovered, picturesque spot along the Oregon coast. The area is nestled between the endless waters of the Pacific and the base of the Neah-Kah-Nie Mountains. For beach roaming, flying kites or just an exhilarating day by the sea, this area is sheer perfection. Manzanita is close enough to Cannon Beach for you to take advantage of all its dining spots and nightlife, and yet far enough from the crowds there to give you a comforting sense of calm.

The inn itself is set amidst coastal pine and spruce and is only 200 feet from a seven-mile stretch of beach. Each unit provides the best in modern conveniences: a private fireside spa, tree-top glimpses of ocean, wet bar with refrigerator, and a generous continental breakfast that is served in your room each day. Plus the rooms are all finished with wood interiors, cushy furnishings and firm cozy beds with down comforters.

◆ **Romantic Suggestion:** There is a charming, small restaurant just two blocks up the street from The Inn at Manzanita. It's a must for an intimate dinner. **JAROBE'S**, 137 Laneda, (503) 368-5113 (Moderate) is open only for dinner, the small interior is adorable, and the menu an interesting blend of Northwest and East Indian cuisine.

THREE CAPES SCENIC LOOP

Before Tillamook you will see signs for Three Capes Scenic Loop. After you turn west off Highway 101, continue following the signs along this loop to Cape Meares, around and south to Oceanside and then down to Netarts.

Highway 101 is inconsistent around here. While it usually offers traveling companions beautiful things to gaze at and admire, it also interrupts your view with crowded shopping areas in towns set far from the water's edge. You can avoid some of this irritation by driving on Three Capes Scenic Loop. Even on the sunniest day in summer, the throngs of tourists seem to be somewhere else and your movement along this exquisite passage through forest and ocean beaches can be taken at a slow, cruising pace. You can stop at dozens of locations to dig for clams or go crabbing. **ANDERSON VIEWPOINT**, a precipitous mountain bluff just south of Oceanside, overlooks everything north, south and west, and is a supreme location for a picnic. At some point during your day's journey you can swoon into each other's arms and toast the views you've enjoyed.

OCEANSIDE

On the Oregon Coast, 8 miles due west of Tillamook on Three Capes Scenic Loop. Follow the signs from Highway 1 just north of Tillamook out to Oceanside.

Much of the Oregon Coast is heavily traveled, especially in the summer — except, that is, for Oceanside. This fairly remote village is about eight miles west of the main road on the small peninsula that creates Tillamook Bay. The drive along this section of the coast, separating you from the crowds, affords plenty of opportunities to stop whenever you see an inviting stretch of rugged coastline. As the mist mingles with the cry of sea birds, you will know for sure that you've left city life behind you, far, far away.

There is nothing fancy in Oceanside; the handful of accommodations range from basic to austere, and there are only two restaurants in the area. But the magnificent Oregon coastline is the reason to be here, with only yourselves and the calm of the moment to concern you.

◆ *Romantic Possibilities:* **ROSEANNA'S RESTAURANT,** 1490 Pacific, (503) 842-7351 (Inexpensive to Moderate), is Oceanside's only oceanside restaurant. Healthy morning breakfasts, lunches and dinners all begin with a bewitching appetizer — the ocean panorama as seen through the windows. Or conclude your day with a dessert splendidly prepared by nature and served up at Roseanna's — sunset.

SEA HAVEN INN, Oceanside

5450 South Avenue N.W.
(503) 842-3151
Inexpensive

From Tillamook follow the signs off Highway 101 to Netarts and Oceanside. Just before you enter the town of Oceanside, follow the signs to Sea Haven on the west side of the road.

This inn is not really a romantic destination. But because Oceanside is such a special location, and there are so few accommodations available here, I feel a responsibility to give you all the options and let you make your own kissing decisions.

The rooms at Sea Haven are very nice and pleasant, but rather on the lackluster side. Although the common areas and outside deck have a wondrous view over the azure ocean and the shoreline far below, most of the rooms are at the rear of the house and have far less expansive views. The innkeeper explained (while she puffed away on her cigarette) that guests are encouraged to mingle and get to know each other, which is nice, but hardly intimate. Breakfasts are well done and generous, and they are served family-style in a dining room area that looks out over the endless miles of empty, mountain-framed beaches.

THREE CAPES BED & BREAKFAST, Oceanside   👄
1685 Maxwell Mountain Road
(503) 842-6126
Inexpensive

Before Tillamook you will see signs for Three Capes Scenic Loop. After you turn west off Highway 101, continue following the signs to Netarts and Oceanside. In Oceanside follow the shoreline on Pacific Avenue. Turn right at the stop sign, then left at the sign indicating Maxwell Mountain Road.

This is not a fancy bed & breakfast. Yet the scenery that fills the bay windows of your homespun room can make any morning or sunset seem a dream come true. The home is situated on the side of a hill overlooking the spectacular Oceanside shore. One of the rooms has a private deck and private entrance.

◆ *Romantic Option:* Up the road from Three Capes Bed & Breakfast is an interesting set of gray, weathered buildings that goes by the name of **HOUSE ON THE HILL**, (503) 842-6030 (Inexpensive). The hill referred to is one of the highest points along the entire coast, and the views from the motel rooms, through floor-to-ceiling windows, are nothing less than awesome. Sadly, the interiors are strictly motel quality, but they are clean and—well, there isn't much else around here.

PALMER HOUSE, Lincoln City
646 N.W. Inlet
(503) 994-7932
Inexpensive to Moderate

From Highway 101 turn west on Sixth Drive and then north on Inlet Avenue to the house.

This new bed & breakfast has everything going for it, especially its stunning hillside location peering out over the shore and the glorious ocean sunsets. There are three lovely rooms, with bathrobes, fireplaces, private entrances, cozy sitting areas, plush white carpeting and ultra-comfortable furnishings. Breakfast is a gourmet presentation of exotic treats prepared by the innkeeper, who is a graduate of the Western Culinary Institute. Ricotta pancakes, peach smoothies, a sorbet meringue called *spuma*, homemade sausages and grapefruit soaked in champagne and Grand Marnier may be waiting for you in the morning. All the rooms have private baths, and there is a common deck area for lounging and gazing at the scenery.

Alas, there is a flaw in all this comfort — part of the scenery is marred by a huge Best Western sign plastered across an even bigger Best Western motel that blocks much of the shoreline. If that detail doesn't get in the way of your amorous requirements, you won't be disappointed with any other aspect of Palmer House.

BAY HOUSE, Lincoln City
5911 S.W. Highway 101
(503) 996-3222
Expensive

Just south of Lincoln City, immediately after you cross the bridge over Siletz Bay, look for the restaurant on the west side of the road.

Bay House is an easy place to pass by. Its weathered exterior, all by itself on a steep bank off the main highway, is hardly what you'd call a showcase. But you will make a major culinary error if you neglect to have an evening meal here while you're touring the Oregon Coast. First, there is the flawless view of Siletz Bay, the driftwood-strewn shoreline, and the flow of the calm clear blue water. Almost every table is blessed with its own share of the lovely scenery. Second, there is the outstanding, exquisite food presented here night after night. The menu is an enterprising assortment of Northwest creations that use fresh local meats and fish. Even the desserts are something to save room for at this fine restaurant.

CHEZ JEANETTE, Gleneden Beach
7150 Old Highway 101
(503) 764-3434
Expensive

From Lincoln City take Highway 101 three miles south to the Gleneden junction, where you turn west onto old Highway 101. Chez Jeanette is a quarter of a mile down the road, the first house on the east side.

This restaurant would delight the most finicky of gourmands. Chez Jeanette is a divinely elegant place that is remarkably cozy and warm. The stone-fronted, homey structure rests snugly against a vine-covered hill and has thick branches curling around its roof and walls. The small dining salon is warmed by two blazing fireplaces that illuminate the softly lit room. Velvety forest-green drapery, lush carpet, regal chairs and wood tables set with bone china and crystal create an atmosphere that satisfies your eyes. After you finish the delectable, creative meal, the rest of you will be satisfied as well. Chez Jeanette's provocative decor and location, intriguing menu and excellent service make it a restaurant designed for romance.

CHANNEL HOUSE, Depoe Bay

P.O. Box 56
(503) 765-2140
Inexpensive to Expensive

In Depoe Bay on Highway 101 look for Channel House signs on the west side of the road that direct you to turn west onto Ellingson Street. The House is at the dead-end.

Don't let the street entrance to Channel House fool you or disappoint you — another existence awaits you inside, once you close the door on your room. Appropriately named, this towering bed & breakfast sits above the turbulent entrance to Depoe Bay. The rocky-cliff setting and venerable coastline are visible from most every room. Some of the more desirable rooms (read *expensive*) have their own private deck, where the steaming hot spa tub is a way to kick back and let go, while you watch the boat traffic file by. The view and hot tub are two reasons for a secluded stay here; another is the handsome, oversize suites that ooze comfort and relaxation. Sit back and let the fireplace warm the sea air while you feel the stress leave your bodies.

OCEAN HOUSE BED & BREAKFAST, Newport

4920 N.W. Woody Way
(503) 265-6158
Inexpensive to Moderate

Call or write for reservations and directions.

If you find yourselves at Ocean House Bed & Breakfast, whether it's a warm summer day or there's a storm blowing in from the north, you will quickly find many reasons to prolong your stay. Perched atop Agate Beach, with a huge lawn and garden through which runs a private trail down to the beach, this bed & breakfast offers plenty of space for stretching out on land or beachcombing at the shore. The windows of the bedrooms upstairs open toward the sea, the downstairs room opens to an outside deck. Superior standards of comfort and care have been upheld over two decades at this sizable country home.

CLIFF HOUSE, Waldport ◖◗
P.O. Box 436 (503) 563-2506
Moderate to Expensive

From Highway 101 just south of Waldport, turn west on Adahi road. Cliff House is a few doors down on the north side of the cul-de-sac.

Everything about Cliff House is extraordinary. The superlative renovation has turned a small seaside home into an intriguing respite from the world at large. Perched on a cliff overlooking thundering surf, this is a location that you wish you could call your own. The interior is covered (and I mean *covered*) with collector antiques and heirlooms, there are vaulted ceilings, knotty pine walls, a grand piano, a beach-stone fireplace and five wonderful rooms with plush linens, chandeliers, and comfy sitting areas. Two of the rooms have their own spacious private decks, and the bridal suite (rated Unbelievably Expensive) has its own spa tub and fully mirrored (including the ceiling) bathroom walls. Outside there is a huge deck with a 180-degree view of everything north, west and east, with a massive hot tub in the center of it with jets that move up and down your spine. Like I said — extraordinary.

There is a caveat about the Cliff House: The proprietors are the most hands-on innkeepers I have ever met. Depending on your perspective, they can border on intrusive. When we returned to our room, our clothes were folded and hung up, our wet bathing suits were dried for us and a personal memento we had packed with us was placed neatly in the center of the carefully turned down bed. The breakfast area, which is large enough to accommodate several small tables for a more intimate morning meal, is arranged with one medium-size table for everyone (except those in the honeymoon suite — they get room service). A stay at Cliff House can be the most pampered getaway the Northwest has to offer, or the most meddlesome. You decide.

THE OREGON HOUSE, Yachats   ◆

94288 Highway 101
(503) 547-3329
Inexpensive

Just 8 miles south of Yachats, directly off Highway 101 on the west side of the road.

The Oregon House is a difficult kissing place to explain because each of the 7 units is so dramatically different, one from the other. Some units have rambling, family-oriented apartment floor plans, others have just one comfortable room overlooking well-kept grounds and a distant piercing blue ocean. One suite, located in the main house, is run like a bed & breakfast (this is the only unit that gets a full-service breakfast in the morning). All the other units, regardless of size, include an assortment of the following: fireplace, skylight, dining nook, deck, patio and full utilitarian kitchen. The Oregon House actually is shaping up to be one distinctive (albeit unusual) place to stay, when you take into consideration the oceanside landscape of rolling lawn heading down to the windswept beach below, the price, and how the owners have greatly improved the place over the past two years.

LA SERRE RESTAURANT, Yachats   ◆◆

Second & Beach Street
(503) 547-3420
Moderate

In downtown Yachats, just off Highway 101 on the west side of the street at Second.

La Serre Restaurant remains one of my favorite dining spots along the Oregon Coast. Unlike most other restaurants along this shore, it is neither Oregon-formal nor rustic American-standard, but a refined, gourmet dining experience with a liberal emphasis on natural, fresh whole foods. The interior design reinforces this image with thriving greenery (unfortunately some of it is fake), oak tables and a wood floor. The service can be slow due to the strain on the kitchen from the popularity of this place, but the wait is well worth it. A meal at La Serre will satisfy your palate, your health awareness and your need to be close to your special someone all at the same time.

◆ *Romantic Note:* If you thought the drive from Cannon Beach to Yachats was awesome, you haven't seen anything yet. The miles between Yachats and Florence are stupendous. The coast is more rugged and mountainous, bordered on the east by the Siuslaw National Forest. The vista turnoffs along this stretch of highway are all located on soaring cliffs that offer arresting panoramas of the coastline due south and north. Take your time during this drive and take advantage of every wayside opportunity for looking and kissing.

WINDWARD INN, Florence

3757 Highway 101 North
(503) 997-8243
Moderate

Just north of Florence on Highway 101, on the west side of the road.

This is a restaurant you have to see on the inside; if you glanced only at the outside you might not give it a second look. There are four separate dining areas here — one for any dining mood you might be in. There is a traditional booth and counter set-up — which is not romantic but great for snacks; a room outfitted with book-lined shelves, wooden tables and windows that look out on the garden; a lounge with an immense 30-foot framed window and a magnificent, massive antique-style oak bar; and the last room is a more formal dining area with a grand piano. Much of the baked goods come from the kitchen, and the diverse menu is really quite tantalizing. If you're near Florence, and it's almost breakfast, lunch or dinnertime, you can find what your appetites need at Windward Inn.

◆ *Romantic Suggestion:* If you're like most Northwesterners, a weekend without a precisely prepared latte, capuccino or espresso is like going without air for too long. I'm not sure how I survived before the advent of this basic necessity of life. My husband and I are sometimes at our romantic best while warming our hands over a hot caffè mocha. Those of you who are well traveled already know that outside of Seattle, Portland, or Vancouver, B.C., the opportunity for maintaining this ritual is chancy at best. Well, not in Florence. **OLD TOWN COFFEE COMPANY,** 1269 Bay Street, (503) 997-7300, (Very Inexpensive) has the art of espresso-making down to a polished science. This earthy specialty café is a breath of fresh-roasted air. Plus you can wander around **OLD TOWN FLORENCE** and browse through the shops and along the riverfront while you sip a steaming brew.

CHARLESTON STATE PARKS, Charleston

The town of Charleston is south of Coos Bay, on a small peninsula 30 miles due west of Highway 101. This trio of state parks south of town is well marked and well worth the detour from the main road. Each of the parks has a distinctive perspective and mood, despite the fact that they are separated only by a few miles.

The first park is **Sunset Bay,** where forest and cool sandy earth flank a small inlet of calm ocean water. The second, further south, is **Shore Acres.** The remains of an estate, on a soaring cliff high above Oregon's coast, this park is renowned for its extensive formal gardens, which are maintained to resemble their former glory. There are numerous lookouts and intriguing paths that ramble over rock-strewn beaches gouged with caves and granite fissures where the water releases its energy in spraying foam and crashing waves. The third park, **Cape Arago,** has less imposing grounds and is more of an everyday picnic spot than its neighbors to the north, except for its disposition high above the shoreline with a northern view of the coast. It is known for its sea lions and harbor seals romping in the surf or sleeping languidly on the rocks.

CLIFF HARBOR GUEST HOUSE, Bandon-by-the-Sea

Beach Loop Road
(503) 347-3956
Moderate

From Highway 101 turn west onto Eleventh Street and then right on Beach Loop Road. Turn left at Ninth Street which is the driveway before the Table Rock Motel.

Bandon-by-the-Sea is one of a few relatively undiscovered seaside towns along the Oregon Coast. Yet the beach here is more spectacular and interesting than at any of the more popular sites further north. The multitude of haystack rocks that rise in tiers from the ocean is awe-inspiring. If you yearn to retreat from the usual, this small beachside community is your answer.

Cliff Harbor Guest House is set atop a cliff overlooking the Bandon shoreline. The rooms each have their own baths and private entrances; one has a stupendous view, kitchen, fireplace and is quite large, the other has a sundeck. Both are nicely done, extremely comfortable and extremely private. There is a feeling of exclusivity about your location. The innkeepers take good care of their guests, and their breakfast of organic ingredients proves it.

◆ *Romantic Note/Warning:* **HILL HOUSE BED & BREAKFAST**, Bandon-by-the-Sea, P.O. Box 1428, (503) 347-2678 (Moderate), I regret to say, has received some bad reports over the past year or so. Of course no one has complained about the view from the rooms or deck, which allows for an unsurpassed front-yard communion with the ocean rarely found along these shores. The comments reflect disappointment that the house has become a bit rundown and unkempt. The large deck that wraps around the front of the home is still a perfect place to snuggle, but the innkeepers are likely to be ever-present, with the television on and one of them smoking. The breakfast has also changed, and not for the better, and that too is regrettable. Perhaps in time this property will return to its former status and Hill House can once again be a recommended hideaway.

◆ *Romantic Suggestion:* Two of the most romantic dining spots for miles around are **INN AT FACE ROCK**, 3225 Beach Loop Drive, Bandon-by-the-Sea, (503) 347-9441 (Moderate), and **LORD BENNETT'S**, 1695 Beach Loop Drive, (503) 347-3663 (Inexpensive to Moderate). The solarium dining room at Inn at Face Rock has a distant view of the water, and the food is good — the fish sometimes outstanding. Lord Bennett's has an excellent, fairly traditional menu and a decent view of the beach, although the windows here are really too small to be effective. Both are contemporary wood structures that were designed to allow the outside to become a vital part of the inside — and with an ocean shoreline this magnificent, that was a very wise thing to do.

Both Inn at Face Rock and Lord Bennett's are associated with accommodations that are very nice and comfortable. Inn at Face Rock has units that are quite pretty, set back a distance from the water; it's more like a condo complex than an inn. **SUNSET MOTEL**, (503) 347-2453, (Inexpensive to Moderate), located next door to Lord Bennett's, has a new oceanfront addition with absolutely stunning views. Both have spas and pools on the property, and the service is orderly and polite.

"Love is, above all, the gift of one's self."
Jean Anouill

OREGON CASCADES

COLUMBIA RIVER GORGE

Oregon's Interstate Highway 84 borders the south side of the Columbia River. Highway 14 runs parallel to it on the north side of the river in Washington state. There are several bridges across the river between Oregon and Washington.

The Columbia River Gorge is a very appropriate entry for this kissing travelog. The 60 miles or so of scenery formed by the river carving its way through the Cascade mountains are a kaleidoscope of heart-stirring images. To travel this passage is to sense the magic afoot in the emerald mountains on the west and blazoned across the sunburnt mountains and grasslands to the east. This is a vast collage of all the intensely beautiful things the Northwest has to offer.

A land so richly endowed by nature is sure to figure in Native American folklore and legends, and the Gorge most cetainly does. There are scads of ponds, mountain lakes, and trails but the waterfalls are undoubtedly the most remarkable natural feature. Depending on the season, they rush to earth in a variety of contours and intensities: Oneonta Falls drops abruptly off a sheer ledge for several hundred feet. Elowah Falls sprays a fine, showery mist over deciduous forest. Punch Bowl Falls pours into crystal clear Eagle Creek. Upper Horsetail Falls is forced out in a jet stream through a portal centered in a wall of rock, and Wahkeenah Falls rushes over rocky steps and beds of stone. Wherever you happen to be in the Columbia River Gorge, its stunning natural pageantry will make you feel that you've found paradise.

♦ ***Romantic Note:*** Though this area is visually stunning, and the trails, natural wonders and fruit-laden countryside are totally splendid, it has yet another attraction — wind surfing. This area has just the kind of reliably exciting air currents that wind surfers relish, and you can watch these enthusiasts and their multicolored sails whip across the Gorge; or get out there and zip over the water yourselves.

THE COLUMBIA RIVER SCENIC HIGHWAY

The 22-mile route starts at the Ainsworth Park exit or the Troutdale exit on Interstate 84 east of Portland.

This highway, the first paved road to cross the Cascades, was constructed in 1915 and is reported to be an engineering marvel. Once you drive this sinuous, moss-covered work of art, you will swear it was really built by wizards. There is none of the commercialism you associate with road travel; you won't be bothered by neon, billboards, superhighways, traffic signs or speeding cars. This scenic highway really accentuates the scenery. In the days when it was built, driving was called touring and cars moseyed along at 30 miles an hour. You can go a tad faster through here now, but not much, and why bother? — you won't want to miss the falls, hikes and roadside vistas that show up suddenly along the way.

◆ **Romantic Note:** During summer, when the kids are out of school, this can be a very crowded strip of road. The best time for romance here is when school is in session.

◆ **Romantic Option:** I don't generally recommend tourist attractions. The crowds associated with them usually prevent intimate moments and privacy. The restaurant in **MULTNOMAH FALLS LODGE**, Bridal Veil, (503) 695-2376, is indeed a tourist attraction, and if it weren't for one unbelievable feature (proclaimed in the lodge's name), this would be just another Northwest wood-and-stone dining room serving three decent meals a day. That attraction, of course, is a plummeting waterfall, spilling for a dramatic 620 feet, almost in the lodge's backyard. This spectacle makes any snack or meal here a momentous occasion.

COLUMBIA GORGE HOTEL, Hood River
4000 West Cliff Drive
(503) 386-5566
Expensive to Very Expensive

One hour east of Portland on Interstate 84, take exit 62 to the hotel.

The wide-ranging grounds of this prestigious Spanish-style villa are on a high, forested bank of the Columbia River with Mount Hood's glacial peak peering through in the distance. The atmosphere is reminiscent of an elegant 1920s country estate, filled with fine crystal, silver, pastel tablecloths and arched bay windows looking over the woods and river. If you plan on being in the neighborhood, make certain your schedule includes a morning stop here. Then get ready for a breakfast extravaganza. From pancakes to biscuits, fresh fruit, eggs and everything in between, this is a morning your stomachs will long remember. The meal is guaranteed to appease every tastebud you possess (and you'll discover some you didn't know about). It is strongly recommended that you prepare yourselves for it the night before. How you prepare is up to you.

The guestrooms at the Columbia Gorge Hotel have finally been redecorated and the result is rooms that are almost as attractive as the restaurant and lobby. Each suite has new Queen Anne-style furniture, floral bedspreads and, at long last, new plush carpeting. Unfortunately, the bathrooms are still the same — not great, but not entirely awful either. It's the pricetag on these accommodations that makes you expect more than what you get here. In any case, this historic landmark deserves the recognition it has achieved over the years.

LAKECLIFF ESTATE BED & BREAKFAST,
Hood River

3820 West Cliff Drive
(503) 386-5918
Inexpensive

Call for reservations and directions.

Rather than staying in the costly accommodations at Columbia Gorge Hotel, consider a sojourn at Lakecliff Estate Bed & Breakfast only a half-mile down, the road from the hotel. This large, beautifully renovated country home is situated on a magnificent, coveted piece of Columbia River property. Almost every room in the house has a commanding view of the river. There is an outside deck at the back of the house that is perfect for lounging and gazing. The rooms are spacious and totally appealing. Each one is a cozy hideaway with thick quilts, stone fireplaces and soft new carpeting. A hearty breakfast awaits you in the morning, making this bed & breakfast an easy place to call home. Sad to say, the rooms do share baths and the dining room table is family-style instead of seatings for two, but the view and the quality of the rooms make those details minor romantic inconveniences and nothing more.

◆ *Romantic Alternative:* If Lakecliff Estate is booked, you will not be disappointed if you find yourselves staying at **STATE STREET INN**, 1005 State Street, (503) 386-1899 (Inexpensive) in the town of Hood River. This immaculate, handsomely renovated English house with gabled roof, oak floors and leaded glass windows that look out to the Columbia River in the distance, is a bright airy place. All the rooms share baths, but for the price, the quality and the delicious breakfast, State Street Inn is a great alternative, especially if romance and wind surfing are high on your list of priorities.

◆ *Romantic Suggestion:* **STONEHEDGE INN**, 3405 Cascade Drive, Hood River, (503) 386-3940 (Moderate to Expensive) is an outstanding place for dinner in Hood River, if you can find it open (hours and days are limited). It is set away from the town area, up a gravel road, surrounded by dense shrubbery that gives no clue to what lies beyond. Once you arrive, this century-old, stone-clad home is an intriguing find. The rooms have been beautifully transformed to accommodate intimate seating, and the food is classic Continental with a Northwest accent. Everything is incredibly fresh and artistically presented.

MANNERING MANOR, Hood River

4112 Sherrard Road
(503) 354-1362
Inexpensive

Call for reservations and directions.

I'm a bit reluctant to recommend this place. The problem is that it's a brand new bed & breakfast with owners who are novice innkeepers, and it seems they aren't exactly clear what they'll be doing with the manor. But if they can make a go of it, and I hope they do, this will be an outstanding kissing location.

Set amidst rolling hills covered with orchards and pristine farmland, this extraordinary home is as stunning in design as it is in setting. The contemporary glass mansion, with a sweeping stone stairway that leads to the entrance, is something to behold — perhaps a bit incongruous in this setting, but nonetheless stately. The two rooms upstairs are huge suites with private baths, towering windows, fireplace in one and a unique wood spa tub in the other. You could easily move in here and never leave. There are three rooms downstairs that share a bath and are very inexpensive places to spend a country weekend. They are smaller then the suites upstairs but still quite nice, upholstered in floral patterns, with wicker touches and windows that peer out to the orchards. Breakfast is as you would expect — generous and every bit as gastronomique as the house.

TIMBERLINE LODGE, Mount Hood

On Mount Hood
(503) 272-3311
Moderate to Expensive

Traveling to Mount Hood from the south, follow Highway 26 up the east side of the mountain. As you near the summit, turn onto Timberline Access road, which will take you to the lodge. From Portland, go east on Highway 26 to

Government Camp, where the Timberline Access road starts its six-mile climb to the lodge.

Mount Hood, like its relative to the north, Mount Rainier, stands as an overwhelming example of nature's potency and formidable genius. Appropriately, near the summit, there rests an example of human creativity, Timberline Lodge. This grand structure is endowed with character and masterful craftsmanship, evidenced in its metal filigree, brick chimneys, steepled rooftops and carved beams. The interior strap-metal furniture, wall murals and intricately arranged wood rafters are further testimony to this artistry. Originally built in 1937, the rooms are beautifully restored, each having an inviting, comfortable decor; some have fireplaces. This handsome lodge and the riveting countenance of Mount Hood together create a scene of rugged romance perfect for two.

◆ **Romantic Note:** In winter, when snow transforms the area into a winter wonderland, the lodge's warmth and the rush of downhill or cross-country skiing make this a sensationally sensual hideaway.

INN AT COOPER SPUR, Mount Hood
10755 Cooper Spur Road
(503) 352-6037
Moderate

Take Highway 26 to Government Camp, where you connect with Highway 35 to Hood River. Nineteen miles past Government Camp, before you reach Hood River, turn left onto Cooper Spur Road. Follow it 2 ¼ miles to the inn.

This restaurant and lodging is best described as a romantic anomaly. It definitely has all the outward signs of a provincial mountain snuggery. At the foot of a gentle, lesser traveled slope, definitely off the beaten bath (about a half hour from the Timberline ski area), a log gateway guards a stone path leading to a charming wood cottage. Inside the restaurant there is more distinctive woodwork, and the aroma of just-baked pies dances about the room. The rooms and cabins have the same type of exterior and the interior is all wood and stone fireplaces. Outside there are almost a dozen hot tubs waiting to soothe tired over-skied muscles. Who could deny how quaint and cozy all that sounds? And it is, but only up to a point. What you discover is that the homey, ultra-basic decor and furnishings and laid-back atmosphere really make this more a place for hiking or ski chums than a haven for starry-eyed lovers. Nevertheless, though this may not be exactly the esoteric destination you were looking for, if it's ski season, Inn at Cooper Spur has mountain hospitality aplenty and all the warmth and social activity you could want.

ROCK SPRINGS GUEST RANCH, Bend
64201 Tyler Road
(503) 382-1957
Moderate to Expensive

On Highway 20 head toward the small town of Tumalo, 10 miles north of Bend. Immediately after you pass the town of Tumalo, look for signs that direct you to the ranch.

Ever since I visited Rock Springs Guest Ranch I have secretly longed to return. The memories of my time there are crystal clear, and when I recall the serenity I came to know during my stay, I feel euphoric.

I got my first impression of the ranch as I drove up the dusty dirt road toward it and saw a grassy meadow full of vigorous horses playing rambunctiously. I knew that I had either truly found the Ponderosa or these were the type of horses you could look at but not touch. I'm a city woman born and raised, and my experience with horses has been at riding stables where the animals look as if they'd rather die than be touched one more time by human hands. At Rock Springs, nothing could be further from that urban reality. These horses adored human contact. They were eager to be tended to and even more eager to challenge the trails and paths that webbed the countryside.

To adequately portray this diamond-in-the-rough location I should probably describe the arresting scenery of mountains and rambling streams, or elaborately detail the accommodations of cabins with fireplaces and large outdoor hot tub and swimming pool. But the essence of Rock Springs Guest Ranch is not revealed by such details; rather, it is revealed when you traverse this land on horseback with someone you love, the breeze cooling your brow in fall and spring, the blush of winter cold on your cheeks, or the balmy summer sun tanning your face while an eagle soars overhead.

As soon as I can get my hands on a parcel of time with my significant other, my saddlebags will be packed and I will return to one of the most inspiring escapes I have found in the Northwest.

◆ **Romantic Note:** The environment at the ranch, especially during the summer, is family-oriented. Plan a visit when school is in session for the optimal romantic atmosphere. Also, the meals are served family-style in the main lodge and are included in the package price.

THE INN OF THE SEVENTH MOUNTAIN, Bend

P.O. Box 1207
(503) 382-8711
Inexpensive to Expensive

Just south of Bend, off Highway 97, follow the signs to the resort.

I am including this one for my husband. He has a rough time feeling romantic when the only thing on the agenda is romance. Given what I do for a living, he gets bored with finding hidden getaways where everything is quiet mountain seclusion or private ocean cottages with glowing fireplaces and huge doses of gentle intimacy. He likes a change of pace once in awhile. He needs a trip down a coursing white-water river, or challenging mountain trails, sturdy mountain bikes, a large pool where rough-housing is considered acceptable, lots of hot tubs, roller skating, horseback riding, a world-class golf course and, of course, excellent restaurants, with a late-night disco just in case we both can't sleep. This turns him on. In fact, with options like this it's hard to turn him off. The Inn of the Seventh Mountain has all these things right at your front door, and more. And most of the rooms, whether efficiency units or suites, have views of the forest and snowcapped Mount Bachelor.

Of course, this isn't what I would call a romantic getaway. The numerous condo-like accommodations are done in a style I'll call "Resort Simplicity," and the pace here is almost always vigorous and busy. In summer the inn becomes the scene for family vacations, and the winter months bring the ski crowd. But off-season, when kids are in school and the first snows are still a few weeks away, this place can almost be called cozy. In any season my husband calls it heaven.

◆ *Romantic Suggestion:* VICTORIAN PANTRY, Bend, 1404 N.W. Galveston, (503) 382-6411, (Inexpensive) is a charming small restaurant, all wood and brick, that serves hearty meals for those in need of nourishment to prepare themselves for the ardors of outdoor activity.

PINEHURST INN, Ashland
17250 Highway 66
(503) 482-1873
Inexpensive

On Highway 66, 23 miles east of Ashland.

Along a country road, a good distance from the nearest city or village, overlooking the forested hills of the Cascade Mountains, this unassuming country inn is just about the most enchanting place to find yourselves in for miles around. The entry room is all cedar and pine with a huge stone fireplace for luxuriant heat. Just beyond that is the restaurant with willow furniture covered in bright floral patterns and lace tablecloths, accented by a rich scarlet-wool carpet. At the front of the dining room is an authentic pot-belly stove that manages to keep everything sultry and warm. From the kitchen comes innovative Northwest cuisine, with fresh ingredients and creative combinations. The menu changes with the mood of the chef and the availability of seasonal vegetables and herbs. Naturally grown beef from local ranches is a specialty, but the chef also has a light hand with fish.

Upstairs there are simple, almost austere rooms with views of the surrounding woods, and surprisingly, each one has a private bath. These rooms aren't exactly suitable for high romance, but the entire experience is unique and serene and the breakfast is superb. If getting away from civilization is what you're looking for — and I mean away — you'll be happy at this location.

◆ **Romantic Note:** Pinehurst Inn has a summer special that includes bed and breakfast and dinner for a price that is less then inexpensive. I don't even have a price category for this romantic bargain. They also have wagon rides that are delightful both summer and winter.

ASHLAND

From Interstate 5 follow the signs to Ashland.

Ashland, Oregon, is a utopian world unto itself — tranquil neighborhoods, dynamic downtown area teeming with shops and restaurants, cosmopolitan nightlife, world-class cultural center, pristine countryside, mountainous terrain bordering fertile river valleys — all, amazingly, located in the middle of nowhere. Not only is the town attractive and its numerous accommodations literally among the best the Northwest has to offer, but the Ashland theatre season, beginning in February and running through October, makes New York City's Broadway pale by comparison. It will take only one visit to make both of you sustaining members of Ashland's annual **SHAKESPEARE FESTIVAL.** If you are not a Shakespeare fan, don't let that stop you; keep in mind that Shakespearean drama is only one component of each season's theatrical offerings. This is one of the largest theatre companies in the United States. You can call the Festival directly for tickets (503) 482-4331, or phone the Southern Oregon Reservation Center, (503) 488-1011 or (800) 547-8052, which is a professionally run ticket agency that can also help you with your reservations.

There is more to do in this small, quaint area than in most any other town in the Northwest. Besides the village activity there is white-water rafting down the Rogue or Klamath rivers, horseback riding, llama hikes, mountain climbing and, during the winter, downhill and cross-country skiing minutes away on Mount Ashland.

◆ *Romantic Note:* Ashland is crowned by the 7,500-foot summit of Mount Ashland. Up here there are over 100 miles of cross-country trails that snake their way through forest, open fields, crystal clear mountain lakes, flowing rivers and rolling hillsides. The views are spectacular. As you glide over endless stretches of white powder you can see the peaks of the Cascades to the north and Mount Shasta at 14,000 feet to the south. The terrain is steep and Mount Ashland is considered to be one of the most challenging downhill mountains around. For skiing information in the area, call the **ASHLAND WINTER RECREATION ASSOCIATION**, (503) 482-8707 or (503) 488-1590.

◆ *Romantic Must:* In the heart of the theatre district is **LITHIA ROSE PARK**, consisting of 100 acres of lawn, forest, ponds, trails, tennis courts, flower gardens, volleyball court and enough space to offer you an individualized section of this lovely playground for yourselves. The immaculate trails eventually become unpaved as they wind their way up to a panoramic view of Ashland and the valley beyond.

COUNTRY WILLOWS BED & BREAKFAST
Ashland

1313 Clay Street
(503) 488-1590
Inexpensive to Expensive

From downtown Ashland take Route 99 east to Clay Street and turn right where the road dead-ends. Go up a short driveway to Country Willows.

I must apologize for omitting Country Willows in the last edition of *The Best Places To Kiss*. That was a big mistake, because this is a truly superior, romantic location.

Country Willows is a forested ranch estate 2½ miles from downtown Ashland. A river flows adjacent to the property and the rushing waters fill the air with soft gentle sounds. Willow trees and pas- ture on which proud horses graze surround the home and renovated barn. The breakfast nook, outside decks, and all the rooms enjoy this view. Each suite is large, with handsome furnishings and hand-tiled private baths, and all are brightly decorated in country fabrics and colors. There is even a huge pool out back with a hot tub that can steam away every care from your city-tired bodies. But the highlight is the newly renovated suite that I call "The Best Place To Kiss." This is a masterpiece of white-stained pinery with a secluded deck overlooking the river, a fireplace, and the most unique built-for-two bathtub I've ever seen. Sunrise is accompa- nied by fresh coffee, homemade breads and whatever creation the inspired innkeepers can think of.

COWSLIP'S BELLE, Ashland
159 N. Main Street
(503) 488-2901
Inexpensive to Moderate

Highway 99 becomes Main Street as you enter the town of Ashland from the northeast or southwest. Cowslip's Belle is on the right side of Main Street, two blocks north of the Shakespeare Festival site.

I found Cowslip's Belle after an infuriating day of 110-degree heat, an overheated car that refused to stay cool unless I ran the heater full blast, and a sunburnt driver's-side arm and thigh that I had to cover with a jacket to keep from blistering. To say the least, in this mood nothing was likely to strike me as romantic. In fact, I was certain that any place I stayed would add fuel to the fire. Only a place like Cowslip's Belle could (and did) facilitate a change of attitude.

Located two blocks from the town and theatre district, this bed & breakfast is where other bed & breakfast owners come to find out how to do it right. Here the attention to your needs is reassuring when things are going wrong and helpful when things are going right. The rooms provide you a great night's sleep on a firm but cushy mattress in a four-poster bed. Sigh with relief as you snuggle under the softest quilts to ever touch your skin. The bathrooms are beautifully done in shiny green and black tiles, and the bedroom furnishings are unique and enviable. At night, when you return from the theatre, there will be homemade, hand-dipped chocolate truffles placed lovingly on your pillows. Breakfast is a fiesta of fruit, French toast, yogurt and home-baked scones.

◆ *Romantic Suggestion:* Ask anyone in Ashland where the best food is served and they are likely to mention **WINCHESTER INN**, 35 South Second Street, Ashland, (503) 488-1113 (Moderate to Expensive). They may also tell you that the restaurant is on the main floor of a renovated Queen Anne-style home where tables are placed casually throughout the library, living room and dining alcove, with plenty of privacy-space in between. The windows look out onto gardens surrounding the building, and the mood is always cordial and relaxed.

ROMEO INN BED & BREAKFAST, Ashland
295 Idaho Street
(503) 488-0884
Moderate to Expensive

From Ashland's main plaza, head south on Main Street and turn right onto Gresham Street. Two blocks down, turn left on Holly and then left on Idaho. The inn is on the corner of Idaho and Holly.

I almost decided to drive right by this one and not check it out. The neighborhood was not the best. Once you're inside, though, the outside melts away and the two of you have all the elements of a romantic interlude.

The home itself is a classic Cape Cod cottage that rests on a hillside dotted with 300-year-old ponderosa pines that fill the air with a sweet, balmy fragrance. There is even a view of the Cascades in the distance. The 5 guestrooms are large, sophisticated, country-style suites. The

Stratford Suite and the Canterbury Room will be of particular interest to those who want a fireplace, hot tub and private entrance.

There is a new addition to this heartwarming place — the Cambridge Suite. It has a vaulted ceiling, tiled fireplace and French doors that open onto a private garden. All the rooms have remarkably comfortable king-size beds and luxurious details. There is even a swimming pool and outdoor hot tub set amidst a well-tended garden. In the morning a generous, conscientiously prepared breakfast is served on bone china, accompanied by freshly squeezed orange juice.

SOARING HAWKS, Ashland

P.O. Box 944
(503) 482-8707
Expensive

Please call for information regarding reservations and directions. A three-night minimum is required.

This was the only kissing place where the owners tried to talk me out of including a description of their house in my book. Their "secluded mountain home" was so precious to them that they didn't want everyone to know about it. I assured them that the readers of *The Best Places To Kiss* were a special type of traveler, looking for places they could cherish, not ravage. That promise made, I am thrilled to describe to you one of the absolute best places to kiss in the Northwest.

The home is an octagonal wood masterpiece, jutting out from the forested slopes of Mount Ashland, with an unparalleled 180-degree view of the Cascade and Siskiyou mountains, with Mount Shasta 50 miles to the south. Special features of the house include a vaulted living room ceiling with a gigantic rock fireplace, floor-to-ceiling windows, a hot tub, a bi-level deck encompassing the entire abode, and top-notch bedrooms with peerless comforts and a priceless view. Located only 16 miles from downtown Ashland and three miles from the ski slopes, the best of all worlds is available at Soaring Hawks.

◆ **Romantic Note:** A minimum three-day stay is required. Also, during the winter the driveway is often impassable, so a 400-foot walk through snow is unavoidable but worth every strenuous step.

◆ **Romantic Alternative:** In the event that Soaring Hawks is booked, inquire into staying down the road at **MOUNT ASHLAND INN**, 550 Mt. Ashland Road, (503) 482-8707 (Moderate to Expensive). This massive, majestic log mansion was designed and built by the same people who created Soaring Hawks. The building itself is an outstanding piece of design work and it's worth a stay if only to see the craftsmanship that went into constructing this mountain retreat. The inn has smaller rooms and the view is less praiseworthy than at Soaring Hawks, but it's also less expensive. Everything is as quaint and cozy as can be, the breakfast is superb, and you are indeed up in the mountains at the heart of the Pacific Crest Trail (the inn is adjacent to it). Each room has a private bath, and the log structure is the finest mountain accommodation you will see anywhere in the region. Not at all a bad option for a bit of mountain intimacy.

CAFÉ AMADEUS, Ashland

120 East Main Street
(503) 488-2446
Moderate to Expensive

On East Main Street in downtown Ashland near First Street.

Inside and out, Café Amadeus is a thoroughly enchanting, totally captivating restaurant, and it is earnestly German. The interior is delightful, with lace curtains and soft pink linens. The entire atmosphere is quaint, with a hint of elegance and a generous dose of charm. If the idea of paprika, bratwurst and schnitzel has kept you from trying German cooking, take down that wall and reconsider your position. All the dishes here are delicate and savory without being heavy. You will leave feeling satisfied, yet light enough to do all the kissing you want. Unless of course you decide to partake in their authentic, delectable Viennese pastries.

◆ *Romantic Option:* **CHATEAULIN RESTAURANT,** 50 East Main Street (503) 482-2264 (Expensive) is a traditional French restaurant with subtle lighting supplemented by flickering candlelight, lace window treatments, scarlet carpeting, and dark woodwork. The seating is intimate, with the accent on tight, almost too-tight table arrangements, particularly just before showtime. Still, the food produced by the serious kitchen is excellent.

◆ *Second Romantic Option:* **IL GIARDINO CUCINA ITALIANA,** 5 Granite Street, (503) 488-0816, (Moderate) is a new restaurant just off Lithia Rose Park. The bright interior and contemporary Italian menu makes it a welcome addition to the Ashland dining scene. The atmosphere is a refreshing blend of formal and comfortable. The pasta dishes are delicious and creative.

CRYSTAL ROOM, Ashland

212 East Main Street
in the Mark Anthony Hotel
(503) 482-1721
Moderate to Expensive

On East Main Street in downtown Ashland, at First Street.

Crystal Room is certainly one of the most fascinating places to dine in Ashland, perhaps in the entire region. Some of its great appeal can be attributed to the food — very French and very good. The fish and meat dishes are prepared with some of the lightest sauce combinations I've ever tasted. And some of the appeal can be attributed to the setting of whitewashed walls, accented with floor-to-ceiling draperies framing the tall windows, and the hand-painted murals à la Toulouse-Lautrec that grace the room and reinforce the classic French atmosphere. The music softly playing in the background almost completes the mood. But the *pièce de la resistance* is the 2,000-pound crystal chandelier that hangs glistening (and I mean *glistening*) in the center of the room. This has to be seen to be believed. There are over 1,200 separate prisms in this antique showstopper, and though it sounds overpowering it really is lovely. Between the food and the setting, Crystal Room is a must. Breakfast here will be a poignant, unforgettable occasion.

◆ *Romantic Option:* HOT ROCK CAFÉ, in the lobby of the Mark Anthony Hotel, is a charming place for dessert, afternoon tea or late-night snack. The setting is traditional European country-elegant with a unique twist — Hot Rock cuisine. The atmosphere sizzles when this one-of-a-kind appetizer is served: you are given fresh prawns, beef tenderloin, vegetable kabob and tequila chicken which you then cook yourself on a fiery hot stone. There are other menu selections if the notion of a do-it-yourself barbecue is not your thing, but you ought to try it once, just for the experience.

◆ *Romantic Warning:* Do not take my enthusiasm for the Crystal Room and the Hot Rock Café at the Mark Anthony Hotel as an encouragement to book a room here. The rooms are most unattractive, complete with sagging beds, sparse, shabby furnishings and inferior linens. And there's a fairly steep pricetag to boot.

*"I sold my memoirs to Parker Brothers
and they are going to make a game out of them."*
Woody Allen

PERSONAL DIARY

This is the section just for the two of you. Here is where you can keep your own record of the romantic, fulfilling moments you've shared together—where you went, what you discovered, the occasion celebrated and whatever else you want to remember long after your adventure has passed. When you're feeling nostalgic, that's the time to read aloud from these personalized pages, to share them as a gift to one another, creating a quiet, at-home magic interlude.

*"Love is the triumph of imagination
over intelligence."*
H.L. Mencken

INDEX

239